Hacking The LSAT

LSAT 70 Explanations

A Study Guide for LSAT 70
(Includes Logic Games Diagrams)

Graeme Blake

ISBN 13: 978-1-927997-00-0
ISBN 10: 1-927997-00-3

Testimonials

Self-study is my preferred way to prep, but I often felt myself missing a few questions each test. Especially for Logic Games, I wanted to see those key inferences which I just couldn't seem to spot on my own. That's where *Hacking The LSAT* came in. These solutions have been a tremendous help for my prep, and in training myself to think the way an experienced test taker would.

- Spencer B.

Graeme paraphrases the question in plain terms, and walks through each step in obtaining the right answer in a very logical way. This book uses the same techniques as other guides, but its so much more consistent and concise! By the time you read through all the tests, you've gradually developed your eye for the questions. Using this book is a great way to test your mastery of techniques!

- Sara L.

Graeme's explanations have the most logical and understandable layout I've seen in an LSAT prep book. The explanations are straightforward and easy to understand, to the point where they make you smack your forehead and say 'of course!

- Michelle V.

"Graeme is someone who clearly demonstrates not only LSAT mastery, but the ability to explain it in a compelling manner. This book is an excellent addition to whatever arsenal you're amassing to tackle the LSAT."

- J.Y. Ping, 7Sage LSAT,
www.7Sage.com

I did not go through every single answer but rather used the explanations to see if they could explain why my answer was wrong and the other correct. I thought the breakdown of "Type", "Conclusion", "Reasoning" and "Analysis" was extremely useful in simplifying the question. As for quality of the explanations I'd give them a 10 out of 10.

- Christian F.

LSAT PrepTests come with answer keys, but it isn't sufficient to know whether or not you picked the credited choice to any given question. The key to making significant gains on this test is understanding the logic underlying the questions.

This is where Graeme's explanations really shine. You may wonder whether your reasoning for a specific question is sound. For the particularly challenging questions, you may be at a complete loss as to how they should be approached.

Having these questions explained by Graeme who scored a 177 on the test is akin to hiring an elite tutor at a fraction of the price. These straightforward explanations will help you improve your performance and, more fundamentally, enhance your overall grasp of the test content.

- Morley Tatro, Cambridge LSAT,
www.cambridgelsat.com

Through his conversational tone, helpful introductions, and general recommendations and tips, Graeme Blake has created an enormously helpful companion volume to *The Next Ten Actual Official LSATs*. He strikes a nice balance between providing the clarity and basic explanation of the questions that is needed for a beginner and describing the more complicated techniques that are necessary for a more advanced student.

Even though the subject matter can be quite dry, Graeme succeeds in making his explanations fun and lighthearted. This is crucial: studying for the LSAT is a daunting and arduous task. By injecting some humor and keeping a casual tone, the painful process of mastering the LSAT becomes a little less painful.

When you use *Hacking The LSAT* in your studying, you will feel like you have a fun and knowledgeable tutor guiding you along the way.

- Law Schuelke, LSAT Tutor,
www.lawLSAT.com

Graeme's explanations are clear, concise and extremely helpful. They've seriously helped me increase my understanding of the LSAT material!

- **Jason H.**

Graeme's book brings a different view to demystifying the LSAT. The book not only explains the right and wrong answers, but teaches you how to read the reading comprehension and the logical reasoning questions. His technique to set up the games rule by rule help me not making any fatal mistakes in the set up. The strategies he teaches can be useful for someone starting as much as for someone wanting to perfect his strategies. Without his help my LSAT score would have been average, he brought my understanding of the LSAT and my score to a higher level even if english is not my mother tongue.

- **Patrick Du.**

This book is a must buy for any who are looking to pass or improve their LSAT, I highly recommend it.

- **Patrick Da.**

This book was really useful to help me understand the questions that I had more difficulty on. When I was not sure as to why the answer to a certain question was that one, the explanations helped me understand where and why I missed the right answer in the first place. I recommend this book to anyone who would like to better understand the mistakes they make.

- **Pamela G.**

Graeme's book is filled with thoughtful and helpful suggestions on how to strategize for the LSAT test. It is well-organized and provides concise explanations and is definitely a good companion for LSAT preparation.

- **Lydia L.**

The explanations are amazing, great job. I can hear your voice in my head as I read through the text.

- **Shawn M.**

Hacking the LSAT, especially the logic games sections, was extremely helpful to my LSAT preparation.

The one downside to self study is that sometimes we do not know why we got a question wrong and thus find it hard to move forward. Graeme's book fixes that; it offers explanations and allows you to see where you went wrong. This is an extremely helpful tool and I'd recommend it to anybody that's looking for an additional study supplement.

- **Joseph C.**

Regardless of how well you're scoring on the LSAT, this book is very helpful. I used it for LR and RC. It breaks down and analyzes each question without the distraction of classification and complicated methods you'll find in some strategy books. Instead of using step-by-step procedures for each question, the analyses focus on using basic critical thinking skills and common sense that point your intuition in the right direction. Even for questions you're getting right, it still helps reinforce the correct thought process. A must-have companion for reviewing prep tests.

- **Christine Y.**

Take a thorough mastery of the test, an easygoing demeanor, and a genuine desire to help, and you've got a solid resource for fine-tuning your approach when you're tirelessly plowing through test after test. Written from the perspective of a test-taker, this book should help guide your entire thought process for each question, start to finish.

- **Yoni Stratievsky, Harvard Ready,** www.harvardready.com

This LSAT guide is the best tool I could have when preparing for the LSAT. Not only does Graeme do a great job of explaining the sections as a whole, he also offers brilliant explanations for each question. He takes the time to explain why an answer is wrong, which is far more helpful when trying to form a studying pattern.

- **Amelia F.**

LSAT 70 Explanations
Table Of Contents

Introduction

The LSAT is a hard test.

The only people who write the LSAT are smart people who did well in University. The LSAT takes the very best students, and forces them to compete.

If the test's difficulty shocked you, this is why. The LSAT is a test designed to be hard for smart people.

That's the bad news. But there's hope. The LSAT is a *standardized* test. It has patterns. It can be learned.

To get better, you have to review your mistakes. Many students write tests and move on, without fully understanding their mistakes.

This is understandable. The LSAC doesn't publish official explanations for most tests. It's hard to be sure why you were wrong.

That's where this book comes in. It's a companion for LSAT 70, the October 2013 LSAT.

This book lets you see where you went wrong. It has a full walk through of each question and of every answer choice. You can use this book to fix your mistakes, and make sure you understand *everything*.

By getting this book, you've shown that you're serious about beating this test. I sincerely hope it helps you get the score you want.

There are a few things that I'd like to highlight.

Logical Reasoning: It can be hard to identify conclusions in LR. You don't get feedback on whether you identified the conclusion correctly.

This book gives you that feedback. I've identified the conclusion and the reasoning for each argument. Try to find these on your own beforehand, and make sure they match mine.

Logic Games: Do the game on your own before looking at my explanation. You can't think about a game unless you're familiar with the rules. Once you read my explanations, draw my diagrams yourself on a sheet of paper. You'll understand them much better by recopying them.

Reading Comprehension: You should form a mental map of the passage. This helps you locate details quickly. Make a 1-2 line summary of each paragraph (it can be a mental summary).

I've written my own summaries for each passage. They show the minimum amount of information that you should know after reading a passage, without looking back.

I've included line references in my explanations. You do not need to check these each time. They're only there in case you aren't sure where something is.

Do these three things, and you can answer most Reading Comprehension questions with ease.:

1. Know the point of the passage.
2. Understand the passage, in broad terms. Reread anything you don't understand.
3. Know where to find details. That's the point of the paragraph summaries. I usually do mine in my head, and they're shorter than what I've written.

Review This Book

Before we start, I'd like to ask you a favor. I'm an independent LSAT instructor. I don't have a marketing budget.

But I do my best to make good guides to the LSAT. If you agree, I would love it if you took two minutes to write a review on amazon.com

People judge a book by its reviews. So if you like this guide you can help others discover it. I'd be very grateful.

Good luck!

Graeme

p.s. I'm a real person, and I want to know how the LSAT goes and what you think of this book. Send me an email at graeme@lsathacks.com!

p.p.s. For more books, check out the further reading section at the back. I'm also offering a free half hour LSAT lesson if you fill out a survey.

How To Use This Book

The word "Hacking" in the title is meant in the sense used by the tech world and Lifehacker: "solving a problem" or "finding a better way".

The LSAT can be beaten, but you need a good method. My goal is for you to use this book to understand your mistakes and master the LSAT.

This book is *not* a replacement for practicing LSAT questions on your own.

You have to try the questions by yourself first. When you review, try to see why you were wrong *before* you look at my explanations.

Active review will teach you to fix your own mistakes. The explanations are there for when you have difficulty solving on a question on your own or when you want another perspective on a question.

When you *do* use the explanations, have the question on hand. These explanations are not meant to be read alone. You should use them to help you think about the questions more deeply.

Most of the logical reasoning explanations are pretty straightforward. Necessary assumption questions are often an exception, so I want to give you some guidance to help you interpret the explanations.

The easiest way to test the right answer on a necessary assumption question is to "negate" it.

You negate a statement by making it false, in the slightest possible way. For example, the negation of "The Yankees will win all their games" is "The Yankees will *not* win all their games (they will lose at least one)."

You *don't* have to say that the Yankees will lose *every* game. That goes too far.

If the negation of an answer choice proves the conclusion wrong, then that answer is *necessary* to the argument, and it's the correct answer.

Often, I negate the answer choices when explaining necessary assumption questions, so just keep in mind why they're negated.

Logic games also deserve special mention.

Diagramming is a special symbolic language that you have to get comfortable with to succeed.

If you just *look* at my diagrams without making them yourself, you may find it hard to follow along. You can only learn a language by using it yourself.

So you will learn *much* more if you draw the diagrams on your own. Once you've seen how I do a setup, try to do it again by yourself.

With constant practice, you *will* get better at diagramming, and soon it will come naturally.

But you must try on your own. Draw the diagrams.

Note that when you draw your own diagrams, you don't have to copy every detail from mine. For example, I often leave off the numbers when I do linear games. I've included them in the book, because they make it easier for you to follow along.

But under timed conditions, I leave out many details so that I can draw diagrams faster. If you practice making drawings with fewer details, they become just as easy to understand.

Keep diagrams as minimal as possible.

If you simply don't *like* the way I draw a certain rule type, then you can substitute in your own style of diagram. Lots of people succeed using different styles of drawing.

Just make sure your replacement is easy to draw consistently, and that the logical effect is the same. I've chosen these diagrams because they are clear, they're easy to draw, and they *keep you from forgetting rules*.

I've included line references to justify Reading Comprehension Answers. Use these only in case you're unsure about an explanation. You don't have to go back to the passage for every line reference.

Short Guide to Logical Reasoning

LR Question Types

Must be True: The correct answer is true.

Most Strongly Supported: The correct answer is probably true.

Strengthen/Weaken: The answer is correct if it even slightly strengthens/weakens the argument.

Parallel Reasoning: The correct answer will mirror the argument's structure exactly. It is often useful to diagram these questions (but not always).

Sufficient Assumption: The correct answer will prove the conclusion. It's often useful to diagram sufficient assumption questions. For example:

The conclusion is: A → D

There is a gap between premises and conclusion:

A   B → C → D   **missing link:** A → B or B̶ → A̶

A → B → C   D   **missing link:** C → D or D̶ → C̶

A → B   C → D   **missing link:** B → C or C̶ → B̶

The right answer will provide the missing link.

Necessary Assumption: The correct answer will be essential to the argument's conclusion. Use the negation technique: If the correct answer is false (negated), then the argument falls apart.
The negation of hot is "not hot" rather than cold.

Point at Issue: Point at Issue questions require two things. **1.** The two speakers must express an opinion on something. **2.** They must disagree about it.

Flawed Reasoning: The correct answer will be a description of a reasoning error made in the argument. It will often be worded very abstractly.

Practice understanding the answers, right and wrong. Flawed Reasoning answers are very abstract, but they all mean something. Think of examples to make them concrete and easier to understand.

Basic Logic

Take the phrase: "All cats have tails."

"Cats" is the sufficient condition. Knowing that something is a cat is "sufficient" for us to say that it has a tail. "Tails" is a necessary condition, because you can't be a cat without a tail. You can draw this sentence as C → T

The **contrapositive** is a correct logical deduction, and reads "anything without a tail is not a cat." You can draw this as T̶ → C̶. Notice that the terms are reversed, and negated.

Incorrect Reversal: "Anything with a tail is a cat." This is a common logical error on the LSAT.

T → C   (Wrong! Dogs have tails and aren't cats.)

Incorrect Negation: "If it is not a cat, it doesn't have a tail." This is another common error.

C̶ → T̶ (Wrong! Dogs aren't cats, but have tails.)

General Advice: Always remember what you are looking for on each question. The correct answer on a strengthen question would be incorrect on a weaken question.

Watch out for subtle shifts in emphasis between the stimulus and the incorrect answer choices. An example would be the difference between "how things are" and "how things should be."

Justify your answers. If you're tempted to choose an answer choice that says something like the sentence below, then be sure you can fill in the blank:

 Answer Choice Says: "The politician attacked his opponents' characters",

Fill In The Blank: "The politician said _____ about his opponents' characters."

If you cannot say what the attack was, you can't pick that answer. This applies to many things. You must be able to show that the stimulus supports your idea.

A Few Logic Games Tips

Rule 1: When following along with my explanations....draw the diagrams yourself, too!

This book will be much more useful if you try the games by yourself first. You must think through games on your own, and no book will do that for you. You must have your mind in a game to solve it.

Use the explanations when you find a game you can't understand on your own, or when you want to know how to solve a game more efficiently.

Some of the solutions may seem impossible to get on your own. It's a matter of practice. When you learn how to solve one game efficiently, solving other games becomes easier too.

Try to do the following when you solve games:

Work With What Is Definite: Focus on what must be true. Don't figure out every possibility.

Draw Your Deductions: Unsuccessful students often make the same deductions as successful students. But the unsuccessful students forget their deductions, 15 seconds later! I watch this happen.

Draw your deductions, or you'll forget them. Don't be arrogant and think this doesn't happen to you. It would happen to *me* if I didn't draw my deductions.

Draw Clear Diagrams: Many students waste time looking back and forth between confusing pictures. They've done everything right, but can't figure out their own drawings!

You should be able to figure out your drawings 3 weeks later. If you can't, then they aren't clear enough. I'm serious: look back at your old drawings. Can you understand them? If not, you need a more consistent, cleaner system.

Draw Local Rules: When a question gives you a new rule (a local rule), draw it. Then look for deductions by combining the new rule with your existing rules. Then double-check what you're being asked and see if your deduction is the right answer. This works 90% of the time for local rule questions. And it's fast.

If you don't think you have time to draw diagrams for each question, practice drawing them faster. It's a learnable skill, and it pays off.

Try To Eliminate a Few Easy Answer Choices First: You'll see examples in the explanations that show how certain deductions will quickly get rid of 1-3 answer choices on many questions. This saves time for harder answer choices and it frees up mental space.

You don't have to try the answer choices in order, without thinking about them first.

Split Games Into Two Scenarios When Appropriate: If a rule only allows something to be one of two ways (e.g. F is in 1 or 7), then draw two diagrams: one with F in 1, and one with F in 7. This leads to extra deductions surprisingly often. And it always makes the game easier to visualize.

Combine Rules To Make Deductions: Look for variables that appear in multiple rules. These can often be combined. Sometimes there are no deductions, but it's a crime not to look for them.

Reread The Rules: Once you've made your diagram, reread the rules. This lets you catch any mistakes, which are fatal. It doesn't take very long, and it helps you get more familiar with the rules.

Draw Rules Directly On The Diagram: Mental space is limited. Three rules are much harder to remember than two. When possible, draw rules on the diagram so you don't have to remember them.

Memorize Your Rules: You should memorize every rule you can't draw on the diagram. It doesn't take long, you'll go faster, and you'll make fewer mistakes. Try it, it's not that hard.

If you spend 30 seconds doing this, you'll often save a minute by going through the game faster.

You should also make a numbered list of rules that aren't on the diagram, in case you need to check them.

Section I - Logical Reasoning

Question 1

QUESTION TYPE: Sufficient Assumption

CONCLUSION: The *Messenger* won't interview Hermann.

REASONING: The *Messenger* won't do anything that its editors think would compromise its integrity. Hermann wants to approve the interview before publication.

ANALYSIS: This is a sufficient assumption questions, not a 'complete the argument' question. The questions asks you to *prove* the conclusion. The way to answer sufficient assumption questions is to arrange the evidence, find the gap, and add a new premise that lets you draw the conclusion.

H wants approval   [gap]   Editor believe compromise integrity → Won't do it

Just put an arrow where the gap is, and you'll see that the missing statement is:

H approval → Editor believe compromise integrity

_____

A. **CORRECT.** Hermann wants the right of approval. This answer shows that the editors think that would compromise the *Messenger's* integrity. And the editors don't do anything if they think it will compromise integrity.
B. The past doesn't guarantee the future. Sure, the editors have never given approval before....but they might change their minds for Hermann.
C. This tells us that most TV stars are different from Hermann. So what? This answer doesn't tell us that the editors will deny Hermann's request.
D. We know exactly *one* reason that the editors will refuse to do something: if they believe that an action compromises their integrity, they won't do it. It's not clear that the editors believe substantial changes will compromise their integrity.
E. This explains why Hermann wants the right of approval. But it doesn't prove that the editors will reject his request.

Question 2

QUESTION TYPE: Flawed Reasoning

CONCLUSION: It's silly to say that GIAPS makes people create bad presentations.

REASONING: GIAPS is just a tool, and therefore isn't responsible for bad presentations. The blame lies with people that use tools poorly.

ANALYSIS: This question is unusual in that the right answer asks you to contradict a premise. The premise is "the tool therefore isn't responsible for bad presentations".

Technically, the premise in question is an intermediate conclusion. It starts with "therefore". All conclusions are fair ground for contradiction, though its rare that the LSAT will require you to contradict intermediate conclusions.

You've probably heard that you're "not allowed" to contradict premises. This isn't true. It's just rare that an answer *actually* contradicts a premise. If you think that an answer contradicts a premise, it's more likely you've misunderstood something.

_____

A. Which claims? There's no inconsistency. To choose this answer, you'd need to find two contradictory claims, i.e. "The software is expensive" and "the software is cheap"
B. The argument didn't say this! Search this question all you want, the author did *not* say anything about good presentations.
C. The argument didn't mention popularity. An answer can't be the flaw if it didn't happen.
D. **CORRECT.** This is a good objection. Maybe the software is really, really bad.
   "So it cannot be responsible...." is an intermediate conclusion and it's not supported by good evidence. That's why it's contradictable.
E. This answer describes an ad hominem flaw. An example is "We shouldn't wear clothes because Hitler wore clothes!". You have to evaluate *what* an argument says, not *who* said it. But this argument doesn't attack anyone's character.

10

Question 3

QUESTION TYPE: Strengthen

CONCLUSION: Alphin Bay shows that there will be damage to the environment.

REASONING: Opponents claim that modern drilling techniques are clean. But drilling began five years ago at Alphin Bay, and it's messy.

ANALYSIS: This is a classic example of a term shift. We don't know what 'modern' is. Drilling at Alphin Bay began five years ago. Were 'modern' techniques used at that time?

Maybe drilling is changing rapidly. If so, pollution at Alphin Bay doesn't prove anything, and the critics might be right.

We can strengthen the argument by showing that Alphin Bay used 'modern' drilling techniques.

_____

A. The argument is about whether oil drilling will *cause* pollution. This answer is about whether we should *allow* pollution. Not the same thing.
B. We care whether the techniques will *actually* cause pollution. Who cares what the company *says*? They could by lying or mistaken.
C. The argument is about whether drilling will cause pollution, not whether we *should* drill.
D. **CORRECT.** If drilling techniques haven't changed in five years, then the techniques used at Alphin Bay were likely modern techniques, too.
   Therefore, this answer tells us that modern drilling techniques would probably pollute the nature reserve as well.
E. So what? The argument is about whether oil drilling will cause pollution. Other industrial activity shouldn't affect whether oil drilling causes pollution.

Question 4

QUESTION TYPE: Point At Issue

ARGUMENTS: James says that community colleges meet the educational needs of their communities, and universities don't.

Margaret says that universities work to serve the communities they're located in. People attend college and university to get a job.

ANALYSIS: This question shifts terms frequently. James says community colleges 'work towards' serving their communities. You can assume that this is the same thing as 'having a goal', which is the language that Margaret uses.

Many topics are only mentioned by one author. For instance, Margaret tells us nothing about the goals of community colleges. And James doesn't tell us why people go to school, so the last half of Margaret's argument is irrelevant.

James says 'educational needs' and Margaret simply says 'needs'. These aren't the same thing; this seems like a minor flaw since the credited answer talks about *educational* needs. However, the question stem just says 'most support', so we don't need 100% proof of disagreement.

_____

A. **CORRECT.** James says community colleges work towards this, but universities don't. Margaret says universities want to serve the needs of their communities. Presumably this includes educational needs.
B. Neither James nor Margaret says whether universities serve educational needs in practice. They both talk about *goals,* while this answer is about what *actually happens.*
C. James doesn't say why people go to university.
D. James doesn't mention the primary educational need in a community, so how could he disagree? For that matter, Margaret also doesn't say what a community's main need is.
E. Margaret agrees, but James has no opinion on this point. So they can't disagree.

Question 5

QUESTION TYPE: Paradox

PARADOX: People who take an organizational seminar tend to become more organized, but they usually don't become more efficient.

ANALYSIS: We associate organization with efficiency, but they're not the same thing. I knew someone who carefully planned every day, and got nothing done.

The best answer will show that the seminar somehow causes people not to gain efficiency.

_____

A. 'Some' is a very vague word, it can refer to one person out of 150,000. Not a useful word in most cases. One person's case can't explain what happens to an entire group.
B. The question talked about people who *do* take organizational seminars. This answer talks about people who do *not* take seminars.
C. This just tells us a random fact about people who take organizational seminars. It's not clear how management training relates to efficiency.
D. This might explain why those people took organizational seminars – those workers knew that they were poorly organized. But this answer adds no information about efficiency.
E. **CORRECT.** Efficiency refers to how much you can get done in a certain amount of time. This answer helps explain why better organizational skills don't make you more efficient: you now have to spend a *lot* of time organizing yourself. So you have less time to actually get things done.

Question 6

QUESTION TYPE: Principle

SITUATION: Some customers incorrectly believed their coupons had expired. This was because the company screwed up. The situation was unfair.

PRINCIPLE: If you cause an unfair situation, you must fix the results of that situation.

ANALYSIS: This question tests your precision. The principle tells you *one* thing. "If you make a bad situation, fix it".

All the wrong answers talk about totally different things. Don't pick an answer because it sounds "reasonable". The answer has to relate to the *one* thing that the principle tells you.

We know that Thimble created an unfair situation. So according to the principle, Thimble must pay. This is a quick way to eliminate answers – anything that says Thimble doesn't need to pay is wrong.

_____

A. Nonsense. We're looking for an answer that forces Thimble to rectify the situation. This answer tells Thimble *not* to give rebates.
B. This answer is about how to assign blame. The principle doesn't tell us how to assign blame. It tells us what Thimble should do if they are guilty.
C. **CORRECT.** This fits with the principle. There's a chance that these consumers failed to get the rebate because of Thimble's mistake. So according to the principle, Thimble must try to rectify the unfair result by giving rebates to anyone who might have missed out.
D. This is insane. Thimble made a promise to give a discount. Rather than tell Thimble to fix the situation, this answer tells Thimble to break their promise, to all consumers. That's *very* unfair.
E. There might be other situations that obligate Thimble to offer a rebate. If someone was unfairly denied a rebate due to ethnic or religious background, then perhaps Thimble is obligated to offer a rebate in that situation too.

Question 7

QUESTION TYPE: Sufficient Assumption

CONCLUSION: The biography doesn't explain what's interesting about Shakespeare.

REASONING: The biography doesn't explain what made Shakespeare different from his peers.

ANALYSIS: The first sentence is the conclusion. If you had trouble identifying this, notice that the conclusion is an opinion. Any idea about whether something is 'good' or 'bad' will usually be the author's opinion. The word "but" in the final sentence indicates evidence for the conclusion.

As with all sufficient assumption questions, there is a gap. In this case, a diagram doesn't help. Just focus: we know exactly *one* negative fact about the book. The book didn't explain what made Shakespeare different.

We want to link that to the idea that the book didn't explain why Shakespeare was interesting. If Shakespeare was interesting *because* he was different, then the single fact proves the conclusion. The thing that made Shakespeare different is also what made him interesting.

A. This might excuse the author's failure to tell us what made Shakespeare different. But it doesn't tell us whether the biography told us what made Shakespeare interesting.
B. Shakespeare wasn't the average man. I have no idea what this answer is supposed to tell us.
C. This might show that the biography *should* have explained why Shakespeare was different. But it doesn't link being different to being interesting.
D. At best this shows that the biography wasn't a good biography. A bad biography might still manage to explain why Shakespeare was interesting.
E. **CORRECT.** This shows that what made Shakespeare different is what made him interesting. So if the biography fails to explain different, then it also fails to explain interesting.

Question 8

QUESTION TYPE: Must be True

FACTS:
1. Whipping cream in a blender produces a crappy, velvety substance.
2. The blender fails because it doesn't let in enough air to whip cream effectively.
3. A special attachment in the blender can help.
4. But the special attachment can't fully compensate for the air intake problem.

ANALYSIS: Must be true questions ask you to combine facts from the stimulus. To do this, you need to have a clear understanding of each fact.

Usually you can't prephrase must be true questions. Instead, you need to load the facts in your short term memory so that you can spot which answer correctly combines two or more facts.

A. There could be *thousands* of methods of whipping cream poorly, and maybe some don't produce the velvety substance that comes from blenders.
B. **CORRECT.** This combines the end of the final sentence with the second sentence. An attachment helps, but it can't change the fact that there isn't enough air in a blender.
C. Be careful of "always". It's a very extreme word. This answer says that an attachment will *never* produce a worse result. That's ridiculous – surely an attachment could malfunction at some point.
D. A very tricky trap answer. The attachment makes things *better*, but maybe to make the result *good* you still need the same quantity of air.

Suppose you need $1500 a month to meet your living expenses, or you'll be all sad and velvety. The moral support of your friends will *reduce* your sadness. But to *solve* the problem you still need the same amount of money, $1500 worth. Moral support can't reduce the money you need.
E. We have no idea which method is the most common. Maybe most people are fools, and use blenders even though they don't work well.

Question 9

QUESTION TYPE: Flawed Reasoning

CONCLUSION: There is good reason to think that the hypothesis is false.

REASONING: There's no evidence for the hypothesis.

ANALYSIS: I intentionally simplified the conclusion and reasoning to make the error clearer. You can't conclude that something is wrong just because there's no evidence to support it. To prove that something is wrong you need actual evidence *against* it.

The astronomer only has *lack* of evidence. He should have concluded "I don't know if the hypothesis is right or wrong. I have no evidence for or against it."

Instead, he assumes that the hypothesis is wrong. When you have no evidence, you can't do that. You have to say "I don't know". Something can be right even if you currently lack evidence that it is.

Don't let the science talk frighten you. Almost all of it is fluff. The entire argument is in the final sentence.

A. **CORRECT.** The astronomer says there is 'good reason' to think that the hypothesis is false. Good reason = evidence. Why does the astronomer think that there is evidence against the hypothesis? In the final sentence, his only proof is that there is no evidence *for* the hypothesis.
B. The astronomer *didn't* say that the hypothesis is inherently implausible. He just said that there's currently no evidence for it.
C. The astronomer didn't mention any hypothesis that is equally likely to be true.
D. Which premises contradict the conclusion? If the flaw didn't happen, then an answer can't be correct.
E. This isn't a flaw. If your opponent makes a true claim, then you *must* grant that it's true, even if it weakens your argument.

Question 10

QUESTION TYPE: Flawed Parallel Reasoning

CONCLUSION: VIVVY is a good program.

REASONING: Three people have had success with VIVVY.

ANALYSIS: This is an unusually stupid argument, though it's very common in advertising.

Suppose that 3,000,000 used VIVVY. Amy, Matt and Evelyn went on to become successful, and the other 2,999,997 students became hobos. Yikes. Would you have your child use VIVVY?

For parallel reasoning, you need to find an abstract way to describe the argument, then find the answer that matches that description. Here, the argument extrapolates from a small sample without indicating how many people the sample was taken from.

A. **CORRECT.** This works. We have no idea how many people play the lottery. It's quite possible that Annie, Francisco and Sean won due to chance and not due to their good luck charms.
B. This is very different. Here, Jesse is in the group of three people, and the conclusion is about Jesse. In the stimulus the conclusion was about everyone.
C. This makes a different error. It confuses necessary and sufficient. Yes, we can expect that those three will be laid off, since everyone hired in the past year will be laid off. But maybe many others will be laid off as well – we can't conclude that these three will be the only victims of layoffs.
D. This is like B. The evidence and the conclusion concerns only the group of three people. In the argument, evidence from three people was used to make a claim about *everyone* who uses VIVVY.
E. This is a flawed argument, but it's a different flaw. Just because *most* people get jobs, you can't say that those three *definitely will* get jobs. Here, evidence from the whole university is used to make a claim about the group of three. In the stimulus, evidence from the group of three was used to make a claim about all users of VIVVY.

14

Question 11

QUESTION TYPE: Argument Evaluation

CONCLUSION: This new sewage sludge fuel technology will help us meet our energy needs with less environmental harm and without nuclear power.

REASONING: The new technology can produce oil from sewage sludge.

ANALYSIS: The stimulus lists an advantage to sewage sludge: it's not nuclear power. But that's all we know.

There are many other questions:

- Does sewage sludge pollute? Several answers address this.
- Is sewage sludge expensive?
- Is there enough sewage sludge to make an impact?

The wrong answer mentions that sewage sludge production has *improved.* I care about whether something is good *now,* not whether it recently got better.

———————————

A. If using sewage as fuel lets us *avoid* dumping sewage sludge, then this technology will be even more useful for protecting the environment.
B. **CORRECT.** It doesn't matter whether the processes have *improved.* That's a relative term. We care whether the processes are currently *good* or *bad.* Those are absolute terms.

   If you get into a car, you care whether it is *safe,* not whether it is *safer* than it used to be. A car could be *safer* and still be a deathtrap.
C. If sewage fuel is too expensive, then it can't replace nuclear.
D. If sewage fuel produces harmful gases, then switching to sewage from nuclear could increase pollution.
E. If sewage fuel produces harmful waste, then it's hard to see how it would be better than nuclear.

Question 12

QUESTION TYPE: Paradox

PARADOX:

1. The most common species reproduce the most, and the rare trees live longer.
2. This is true no matter which species is common and which is rare.

ANALYSIS: Your first task on paradox questions is to understand the paradox. Let's imagine that there are only two trees in forests: spruces, and elms.

- In one forest, spruces are most common, and elms live longest.
- In another forest, elms are most common, and spruces live longest.

So it's not some feature of each tree species that causes them to live longer. It's the fact that trees are rare that seems to cause them to live longer. The species that reproduces best within a forest is also the shortest lived. That seems odd, and it's what you have to explain.

———————————

A. This explains why one species is more common, but it doesn't explain why the rare species lives longer.
B. This explains nothing. It doesn't tell us why trees live to be old in the first place.
C. Good, this shows the scientists were smart enough not to introduce an uncontrolled variable into their experiments. But this doesn't *explain* anything, it just means that the experiments were well done.
D. This shows that it is *useful* for the rare species to survive. But that doesn't explain *why* they survive. Plenty of useful things never happen.
E. **CORRECT.** If there's more competition, then we can expect some trees of the more common species not to have enough resources, and to die. The rare species are living a life of luxury, as there's little competition for resources. Thus they live longer.

Question 13

QUESTION TYPE: Necessary Assumption

CONCLUSION: The TV station's ad is worse than the producers' ad.

REASONING: The TV station's ad is grossly misleading.

ANALYSIS: This is a classic LSAT error. It makes a comparison, but only tells you about one of the two ads.

The argument tells us that the station's ad was grossly misleading. But the argument doesn't tell us anything about the producers' ad. The argument merely *implies* that the producer's ad wasn't also grossly misleading. So the argument merely *assumes* that the producers' ad is better.

————————

A. The stimulus wasn't about how viewers discover the program. The stimulus was only about how effective each ad would be.
B. CORRECT. The negation of this answer wrecks the argument. There's no difference between the ads if this answer isn't true.

    Negation: The producer's ad would have been grossly misleading as well.
C. Same as A. The stimulus is not about how most viewers found the program. The argument is about whether or not the TV station's ad was effective, compared to the producers' ad.
D. This goes too far. The stimulus didn't say that the producers' ad was the greatest ad in the history of the known universe. The argument only said that the producers' ad would have been *better* than the TV station's ad.
E. Same as A and C. The stimulus was about whether the TV station's ad was worse than the producers' ad. This answer doesn't even talk about the ads, it just gives us a useless fact about the audience.

Question 14

QUESTION TYPE: Principle

SITUATION: Sharon's favorite novelist criticized a political candidate that Sharon supports. Sharon decided that the novelist was not so smart, and kept her opinion of the political candidate.

ANALYSIS: This principle question gives you an individual situation. You need to find a principle that matches the information in this stimulus.

Sharon seems to trust her political candidate more than she trusts the novelist. That's about all we know. She liked both the writer and the candidate for a long time, but supported the politician when the two of them disagreed.

There are a few possible interpretations:

* Given a choice between a long favored novelist and a long favored politician, some people will choose the politician.
* If someone contradicts your opinion, you'll probably disagree with them and stick to your opinion.

————————

A. This isn't supported. Sharon was one of the novelist's most dedicated fans, yet she wasn't influenced by the novelist.
B. This is far too broad. It matches none of the elements of the stimulus, and it tells us that we should almost always reject the political opinions of artists. But Sharon might have listened to the novelist if she hadn't been a long term supporter of the politician.
C. This is too broad. We don't actually know that the artist was wrong to speak out. The novelist lost Sharon's support, but maybe many others agreed with the novelist.
D. CORRECT. This works. Sharon had supported the politician for a long time. The novelist contradicted her. Rather than reassess her opinion, Sharon rejected the novelist.
E. This doesn't work. Sharon's allegiance to both the novelist and the politician was longstanding.

Question 15

QUESTION TYPE: Flawed Reasoning

CONCLUSION: Sparkle Cola was the best cola.

REASONING: The participants were evenly divided into five groups. Most people preferred Sparkle cola.

ANALYSIS: This tests your understanding of the word 'most', and your ability to visualize five different groups. I'll use an analogy. Let's say that we're determining the highest rated food. There are five groups, and each group is given the choice between spinach and one other food. Here are the alternate choices for each group, numbered 1-5:

1. Liver
2. Garbage
3. Rotten meat
4. Jellyfish
5. Ice Cream

Bleuck! Ugh! Ewww! Ick! ....Yum!

Groups 1-4 choose to eat spinach. They hate it, but the alternative is worse. Group 5 chooses to each ice cream, and loves it. So 'most' people chose spinach, but ice cream was the most highly rated food.

A. **CORRECT.** It's possible that one group had the cola of the gods, Ambrosia-Coke. They *loved* it, and preferred it to Sparkle Cola. The other groups preferred Sparkle cola, but gave it a low rating. Ambrosia-Coke got the highest rating of any of the colas.
B. The argument didn't say anything about what the volunteers would *buy*. An answer can't be a flaw if it doesn't happen.
C. This isn't a flaw! The study compared sparkle cola to other colas. The study didn't claim that sparkle was the best cola in the world. The ad just said that Sparkle was the best in the study.
D. This answer tests whether you read the question. The volunteers were *blindfolded!* Obviously, they didn't choose colas based on packaging.
E. So? The study was just a comparison of *colas*. You don't need to ask people about wine or milk when you're studying their cola preferences.

Question 16

QUESTION TYPE: Weaken

CONCLUSION: TV makes people overestimate risk.

REASONING: There is a correlation between how much TV someone watches and how likely they think they are to suffer from a natural disaster.

ANALYSIS: Repeat after me: correlation does not equal causation. Correlation does not equal causation. Correlation does not equal causation.

Anytime two things happen together, that's just a *correlation*. In this stimulus, we have two things happening together: TV watching, and fear of natural disaster. Here are the four possibilities:

1. TV causes fear
2. Fear causes more TV watching
3. A third factor (e.g. living in a certain area) causes both fear of disaster and TV watching.
4. It's just a coincidence

You can weaken an attempt to draw causation from correlation by showing that one of the alternate possibilities is true. In this situation, it's also possible that TV watchers are the ones with a correct view of the risk of natural disaster, and therefore TV isn't misleading.

A. So? This doesn't show that TV doesn't cause fear.
B. This heightens the tension. The people who watch the most TV have the greatest fear of natural disasters AND live in the regions with the fewest disasters.
C. Tempting, but this is talking about the wrong group. If this answer had said that people who watch more TV have an accurate view, then *that* would weaken the idea that TV misleads.
D. This shows that Television isn't responsible for educating people about natural disasters. So this answer doesn't weaken the idea that TV is a bad influence.
E. **CORRECT.** This is number three from my list above. A third factor (risky location) leads people to watch lots of television, and to have an above average estimation of natural disaster risk.

Question 17

QUESTION TYPE: Role in Argument

CONCLUSION: Heavy rains will happen more often if the earth's atmosphere becomes much warmer.

REASONING: A warm atmosphere leads to:

1. Warmer oceans, which cause fast evaporation, which means rain clouds form more quickly.
2. More moisture and larger clouds.
3. Large clouds lead to heavier downpours.

ANALYSIS: You don't need to get too technical for role in argument questions. Just identify the conclusion and premises. The conclusion is the first sentence. The fact that it says "likely" indicates that it's probably an opinion and thus the conclusion.

The stimulus lists three facts to support the conclusion. You can combine the facts into one statement: "Warming will cause faster accumulation of large clouds that cause heavier downpours". This statement supports the slightly more direct idea that a warm atmosphere leads to more heavy rains.

The sentence in question is just a fact. The term "in general" is a clue: it's not a conclusion indicator.

A. The first sentence is the conclusion.
B. The first sentence is the *only* explicitly stated conclusion. Explicitly stated = written down.
C. This answer tempted me. But to choose this, you'd have to say which of the first two facts supports the third. Neither of them do: the third fact stands on its own and doesn't need support.
D. **CORRECT.** See the explanation above. The three facts stand independently of each other, and combine to support the first sentence, which is the conclusion.
E. Nonsense. There was no phenomenon in the conclusion, only a prediction of a phenomenon. So the premises don't explain the phenomenon. Instead, they support the likelihood of the prediction. That's the second way to eliminate this answer: the third sentence definitely supports the conclusion.

Question 18

QUESTION TYPE: Identify The Conclusion

CONCLUSION: Anthropologists overrate the usefulness of field studies.

REASONING: Living in a community affects that community, and anthropologists underestimate how much communities are affected.

ANALYSIS: The word 'however' is *very* important in arguments. It indicates two things:

1. Contrast with what was said before.
2. The author's opinion.

Author's opinion = the main conclusion. Usually, anyway. So typically, the phrase that follows "however" is the conclusion. That's all you need to know for this type of question.

The first sentence provides context. The final sentence shows *why* anthropologists overrate field studies.

Note that the argument is *not* claiming that field studies aren't helpful. The claim is that they are overrated: i.e. They're not *as* helpful as they seem.

Note: Sometimes, the phrase after "however" is evidence for the conclusion. In those cases, the conclusion will directly follow, after a word like "so".

E.g. "However, I don't like the opera. *So,* I won't be using the free tickets."

A. **CORRECT.** See the explanation above. "However" indicates the conclusion in this case.
B. This is just context that tells us about field studies.
C. Same as B. This is just context.
D. This is just a fact that shows anthropologists aren't completely clueless.
E. This is the main premise that supports the conclusion. *Because* anthropologists underestimate their own impact, they *therefore* overestimate the usefulness of field studies.

Question 19

QUESTION TYPE: Parallel Reasoning

CONCLUSION: The proposal will probably be rejected.

REASONING: Juarez says:

Not rewritten → Rejected

Two facts:

1. Juarez is very reliable.
2. The proposal won't be rewritten.

ANALYSIS: This is a good argument, with a unique structure. Juarez makes a conditional statement.

The argument says that we can trust Juarez, and it says that the sufficient condition of the conditional statement is true. The conclusion is probabilistic, not certain.

So look for an answer that matches this structure. This is the key to answering long parallel reasoning questions quickly. You can skip over answers that don't seem to match. I'll point out the structural differences that let you quickly eliminate answers.

A. Here, the science journal (i.e. Juarez) provides a fact, not a conditional statement. Wrong! Next answer, please.
B. Same as A. The science journal provides a fact, not a conditional. Also, we don't have the same probabilistic conclusion. This argument concludes that the medication is *definitely* safe.
C. **CORRECT.** This mirrors the structure exactly. Science Journal says:

Data accurate → Drug Safe

Two facts:

1. Journal usually right.
2. Data accurate.
D. Here the journal made *two* claims. Juarez made one. Wrong! Next answer, please.
E. Here the journal states a fact. Juarez stated a conditional. Wrong!

Question 20

QUESTION TYPE: Flawed Reasoning

CONCLUSION: Most people could save hundreds of dollars by switching to Popeka.

REASONING: People who have switched to Popeka saved hundreds of dollars on average.

ANALYSIS: The LSAT expects you to understand the scientific method. One key to science is that samples should be *random*.

The sample here is not random. The people who saved hundreds of dollars *chose* to switch to Popeka. Maybe they switched *because* they knew they would saved hundreds. Maybe the people who haven't switched to Popeka would *not* save hundreds, and that's why they don't switch.

To put it another way, imagine I run a program called "Auto insurance for Bob". Anyone named Bob can save $1,000 with my program. So the average savings is $1,000, because only Bobs enroll in my program. But this Bob-related evidence doesn't prove that Jim will save money if he switches.

A. 'Some' is a useless word. Drill this into your head. 'Some' can refer to 1-2 people. Who cares if 1-2 people didn't save money. Thousands of others might have saved money!
B. The first test of whether an answer is the flaw is: did this even happen? This answers says "if you're new, you pay as much as older customers". The argument didn't say or assume that! So this can't be the flaw.
C. Who cares? This isn't a flaw. The conclusion is "Popeka will save you money". The argument didn't claim that "Popeka will save you more money than any other company will".
D. If policyholders underreported their savings, then the argument is *stronger*. The actual savings would be higher, which supports the conclusion. This is not a flaw!
E. **CORRECT.** This means "People switched to Popeka *because* they could save money". Maybe others don't switch because they know they can't save money. See the explanation above.

Question 21

QUESTION TYPE: Necessary Assumption

CONCLUSION: Front-loading machines require a special detergent in order to properly clean clothes.

REASONING: Ordinary powder detergent doesn't fully dissolve in front loading machines.

ANALYSIS: Pay close attention anytime terms switch, especially when it seems "reasonable" to assume that they mean the same thing.

The evidence is that "powder won't dissolve fully". The conclusion is that "clothes won't get fully clean". That sounds reasonable, but who says powder needs to dissolve fully in order to clean clothes? That's just an assumption the argument is making.

A. Negate this: "One top loading machine in Mongolia uses half an ounce more water than other top loading machines". That certainly doesn't wreck the argument.
B. Negate this: "A detergent designed for front loading washers also dissolves well in top loading washers". That just shows that the detergent can work in both types. Great!
C. This answer refers to all washing machines. So you could negate it by saying "Front loading machines require special detergent, but top loading machines can use any kind". The argument is only about front loading machines.
D. **CORRECT.** I don't think this answer is properly formulated. I think it should have said "An ordinary powder detergent does not get clothes really clean unless it dissolves readily". You could negate the answer as written by saying that liquid detergent doesn't need to dissolve readily, but powder detergents do. That wouldn't wreck the argument. That said, this is the best answer. **Negation:** A detergent can get clothes really clean even if it doesn't dissolve readily.
E. We know that top loading washers use more water, and they may get clothes cleaner with ordinary detergent. But that doesn't mean that more water is *always* good. Maybe there's a washer that uses *even more* water but doesn't work well.

Question 22

QUESTION TYPE: Must Be True

FACTS:
1. Most physicians don't think that they're influenced by gifts.
2. Most physicians think that other physicians are influenced by gifts.

ANALYSIS: This question tests a rare deduction. If you combine two most statements, they have to overlap, and you can conclude a 'some' statement. I'll prove it with a small example. Let's imagine three doctors: Smith, Lopez and Dietrich.

There are just three doctors, so two out of three of them equals 'most' doctors. So let's say that Smith and Lopez both believe that the other two doctors are guilty AND let's say that both Smith and Lopez believe that they themselves are innocent.

- People who think they are innocent: Smith, Lopez
- People blamed by other doctors as being influenced: Smith, Lopez, Dietrich

Obviously, someone is wrong. Every doctor has been accused of being influenced, yet two of them believe they aren't influenced.

And that's exactly what we can conclude. At least some doctors are wrong.

A. We have no idea what effect gifts actually have. The stimulus only gives us evidence about physicians' *beliefs*.
B. The stimulus doesn't mention guidelines. A 'must be true' answer must be based on something from the stimulus.
C. **CORRECT.** See the example above. There are at least some doctors who believe that they are innocent and yet are accused by some other doctors.
D. The stimulus never mentioned *any* physicians who admit that they were influenced. We only know that 'most' physicians think that they are innocent: most can mean 'all'.
E. Same as D. We have no proof that any physicians admit guilt.

Question 23

QUESTION TYPE: Principle – Strengthen

CONCLUSION: The country is not a well-functioning democracy.

REASONING: Most people want the bill, but influential people oppose it. The bill won't violate human rights.

ANALYSIS: Principle questions are sometimes like sufficient assumption questions. The stimulus will give you a bunch of facts, then give a moral judgment. You need to show that those facts justify the moral judgment. So we need an answer that says one of the following:

Well functioning → pass into law if benefits and no violations within a few years

NOT pass into law if benefits and no violations within a few years → NOT well functioning

Be very precise. Two wrong answers sound good, but have the wrong timeline.

A. This is almost right. But the stimulus said most people *favored* the bill. This answer talks about bills that *benefit* most people. Those are different things.
B. This sounds good, but look at the timeline. The stimulus complained that the bill wouldn't be passed into law for a few years, but it might be passed eventually. So the situation might not violate the criterion in this answer choice.
C. This answer supports the idea that we *are* in a well functioning democracy. It says that it's normal for such a democracy not to pass useful bills if influential people oppose them.
D. This describes bills that *are* passed. The question was about a bill that is *not* going to be passed.
E. **CORRECT.** This answer fits the facts. It says that in a well functioning democracy, beneficial bills will be promptly passed into law. In the stimulus, the beneficial bill wouldn't be passed for a few years, if at all.

Question 24

QUESTION TYPE: Must Be True

FACTS:

1. Most commercial fertilizers just have macronutrients.
2. Plants also need micronutrients.
3. Raking grass removes micronutrients.

ANALYSIS: You can combine all three statements to say:

"If grass is raked away, then commercial fertilizers alone won't be enough to keep plants healthy"

That's all we know. All the wrong answers mix up sufficient and necessary.

A. The stimulus said that the most *widely available* fertilizers only have macronutrients. But there could be some less common fertilizers that include micronutrients as well.
B. This answer reverses sufficient and necessary. The stimulus says that commercial fertilizers are a *sufficient* condition for having macronutrients. But other things could also have macronutrients. Heck, you can buy potassium pills.
C. **CORRECT.** This combines all three facts. If you rake away grass, then the soil will be missing micronutrients. Yet most commercial fertilizers don't contain micronutrients.
D. This is very tempting. Its true that commercial fertilizer + grass clippings seem like a *sufficient* condition for soil health. But this answer says that they are a *necessary* condition. We don't know that. Maybe soil doesn't need commercial fertilizers – forests don't need fertilizer.
E. If you rake up grass clippings, your soil will lack micronutrients, true. But there might be ways to restore micronutrients.

Question 25

QUESTION TYPE: Strengthen

CONCLUSION: Manufacturers can't dilute their waste to bring it below the acceptable level.

REASONING: No reasoning was given.

ANALYSIS: The question is quite specific. It asks us to justify the anti-dilution provision mentioned at the very end. Most of this stimulus is just fluff. The stimulus didn't give any justification for the rule that stops manufacturers from diluting their waste.

So practically any reason will do. You just have to identify which answer gives us a reason not to dilute waste. Only two answers even mention diluted waste, and only answer C mentions that diluted waste can be harmful, so it's correct.

A. This explains why we should be careful with waste. But the question asks about the anti-dilution provision, and this answer doesn't address that.

B. **CORRECT.** "Undiluted" in this case refers to waste that has more than 500 parts per million. You wouldn't bother describing waste as undiluted if it didn't have a high concentration. This answer shows that diluted waste is still harmful. If you group a bunch of it together (say, by putting it in a dump) then it's dangerous.

C. This reduces the risk of XTX. It doesn't help explain why we shouldn't allow the dumping of diluted XTX waste. We need an answer that shows a *danger*.

D. This explains why dump owners won't accept undiluted waste. But the question asks about a law that prevents us from dumping *diluted* waste.

E. This explains why manufacturers might want to dilute waste. It doesn't explain why the law prevents them from diluting waste.

Section II - Reading Comprehension
Passage 1 - Prion Pathogens
Questions 1-7

Paragraph Summaries

1. Scientists used to assume that pathogens had DNA in their cell structure.
2. CJD is caused by prions. Prions are a pathogen composed mostly of protein. They have no nucleic acid or genetic material in their cell structure.
3. **First half of 3rd paragraph:** Prions are normal cells. But they can go weird, become dangerous, and replicate themselves. This replication creates a plaque that kills nerve cells. **Second half of 3rd paragraph:** The immune system can't fight prions, as they are normal cells. So there's no way to stop prions, and CJD is fatal.
4. Scientists were skeptical of prions, but now they accept that prions cause CJD and maybe other diseases. But we don't really understand the mechanisms by which prions replicate and destroy cells.

Analysis

This is a very dense passage. If you dislike science then you probably weren't happy to see this first. If you find scientific language off-putting, I recommend checking out ~20 back issues of the Economist from the library. Each issue has about three pages of well written science articles. Reading them is an excellent way to become familiar with scientific language and concepts.

Another good idea is to reread any sections of the passage that you don't understand. I've timed students, and they greatly overestimate how much time it takes to reread a paragraph. When you read something twice you understand it much better and you can go faster on the questions.

The gist of this passage is that prions are a new type of pathogen. Pathogen just means something that causes disease.

We used to think that all pathogens had DNA (also known as nucleic acid). But prions don't have DNA (line 22). This is the most important fact in the passage, so **I'll repeat it: Prions lack DNA.**

Prions sound pretty nasty. They're ordinary proteins in your body, so your immune system won't attack them (lines 40-42). Unfortunately, sometimes prions go wonky and get a strange shape (lines 29-30).

When prions take this new shape, they start reproducing. Scientists aren't really sure how prions reproduce (lines 58-60), but the result is quite deadly.

The immune system can't stop the prions, and we haven't found therapies to stop them, either. So prions just keep reproducing, and eventually kill you (line 45).

CJD is the main disease mentioned in the passage, and it's caused by prions. When prions in the brain reproduce, they create a plaque that kills nerve cells (line 39).

A few answer choices talk about prions being contagious. This is a red herring. The passage never says if prions can spread from person to person. Line 31 mentions that prions are "infectious", but this just means that prions spread quickly *within* your body. If prions spread to someone else, that person's immune system would likely attack the prions, because immune systems attack things that come from outside the body.

It's important to note that we're not *sure* about much. The theory of prions as disease agents is fairly well supported (lines 50-56), but we don't fully understand prions (lines 56-60). We're not even 100% certain that prions cause CJD. The passage is not clear on this point, but lines 12-15 say that the prion theory has merely *challenged* conventional wisdom. Researchers haven't yet definitively proven that conventional wisdom is wrong.

Question 1

DISCUSSION: The main point of the passage is that prions are a newly discovered pathogen that cause CJD and other diseases. Prions are special because they replicate but don't have DNA.

_____

A. This isn't even true. The passage never mentioned whether most organisms can produce several kinds of protein. Also this answer completely ignores disease, which was a major focus of the passage.
B. CORRECT. This covers all the main points: disease and a new way for pathogens to replicate.
C. This just covers part of the final paragraph. A main point answer should cover the whole passage.
D. This answer covers only a few words: the first half of the first sentence of the final paragraph. The rest of the passage doesn't talk about scientific skepticism. Indeed, it seems that now scientists accept prion theory. See line 52.
E. This is just a small part of the passage. This answer completely ignores disease and pathogens.

Question 2

DISCUSSION: On this type of question, narrow it down to 1-2 answers, then check the passage for confirmation. You can almost always prove a 'most strongly supported' question by reference to the passage.

_____

A. CORRECT. Lines 9-11 say that scientists traditionally believed that pathogens had DNA. The rest of the passage says that prions are a pathogen that has no DNA yet causes CJD.
B. The passage never mentions how CJD spreads or if prions are contagious. The passage implies that prions aren't contagious, because they are produced within *our* body (line 40). That's why our immune systems don't attack them.
  If your prions entered someone else's body, their immune system would likely react. You *can* use outside knowledge to make warranted assumptions: we know immune systems often reject foreign tissues.
C. Unfortunately, we don't really understand why prions reproduce and cause disease (lines 57-60), so we don't know how to stop CJD.
D. Lines 45-47 directly contradict this answer. There are wide variations in how the disease progresses.
E. Lines 50-51 make clear that the prion theory of CJD now has considerable support. There was only *initial* skepticism.

Question 3

DISCUSSION: This question says that the passage helps to answer the question asked by the right answer.

So you should narrow things down to 1-2 answers, then check that the passage actually *does* answer the question in the answer choice you choose.

———————————

A. We don't know what causes prions to replicate (lines 56-60), so it's not clear whether blows to the head are relevant.
B. *Chronic* insomnia is a symptom of CJD (line 19), but *occasional* insomnia isn't mentioned as a symptom. Lots of people have occasional difficulty sleeping.
C. Radiation or gene damage isn't mentioned in the passage. Heck, prions don't *have* genetic material. See line 22, prions lack nucleic acid.
D. The passage never says whether heredity is risk factor for CJD.
E. **CORRECT.** Lines 36-39 show that prions damage the brain by creating thread like structures.

Question 4

DISCUSSION: Another specific detail question. As with questions 2 and 3, you can answer this by referencing a specific line in the passage.

If you don't do this, you *will* make mistakes. With practice, it only take 5-10 seconds to confirm your answer and achieve 100% certainty.

———————————

A. The passage never talks about transmitting CJD. And the passage implies that prions aren't contagious. The immune system doesn't attack them because they are part of the body (line 40). But the immune system normally attacks things that come from other people's bodies, such as transplanted organs.
B. This goes too far. The point of the passage is that prions are pathogens, and therefore not *all* pathogens replicate via DNA. But it still could be true that most pathogens have DNA.
C. **CORRECT.** Lines 30-40 support this. Prions are dangerous because they reproduce within the body and create plaque. The plaque kills nerve cells. Without replication, prions couldn't create plaque.
D. Lines 54-56 only say that prions *may* be involved in Alzheimer's and Parkinson's disease. We can't say for certain what causes those diseases, so this answer isn't supported.
E. The passage never compares the aggressiveness of prions to other pathogens. It's true that CJD is fatal, but that's not because CJD is particularly aggressive. It's because we have no defense against prions. So they have all the time in the world to kill us.

Question 5

DISCUSSION: I was stuck on this question, because I forgot that it was a LEAST likely question. Make sure to double check question stems if you're stuck.

For this type of question, if you're stuck between two answers: remember that all the wrong answers can be eliminated by reference to the passage.

A. This is very well supported. Abnormal prions are the ones that replicate and cause CJD (lines 30-40).

B. CORRECT. Unfortunately, line 45 says that CJD is *always* fatal.

C. Line 22 supports this. Prions lack nucleic acid, yet they still reproduce.

D. Lines 40-42 support this. Our immune system doesn't attack prions, and the passage doesn't mention any other natural defenses.

E. Lines 56-60 support this.

Question 6

DISCUSSION: A pathogen is something that causes diseases and replicates itself (lines 2-5). Prions appear to be pathogens (see lines 19-24).

We used to think that pathogens had DNA, but prions lack DNA (see line 22).

This question asks us to assume that all the facts we learned about prions are true. Remember, we're looking for things that must be false. It's possible that certain answers *could* be false, but that's not enough. B and C aren't necessarily true, for instance, but they could be true, and that's all you need.

A. CORRECT. The contrapositive of this answer is: pathogens have nucleic acid. But the theory says that prions are pathogens and that they lack nucleic acid (line 22). So this answer contradicts the passage.

B. This seems true. The passage implies that the discovery of prions was recent.

C. Lines 1-3 support this. Pathogens are things that cause disease.

D. If the prion theory is correct, then prions are pathogens, and prions cause CJD. So this answer would be true.

E. This seems true. If the prion theory is correct, then prions are also pathogens. Prions are not bacteria, viruses, fungi or parasites.

Question 7

DISCUSSION: Scientists haven't proven that prions cause CJD. They've just noticed a correlation. Prions replicate, and CJD progresses. This isn't *extremely* clear in the passage, since the third paragraph indicates that prions are definitely the cause. But paragraphs 2 and 4 make clear that there's still some doubt about whether prions actually cause CJD. See lines 48-52 (They say the experiments "*supported* the conclusion"....not *proved*), and lines 12-14 (They say that the "assumption has been *challenged*"....not *disproven*).

So there may only be a correlation between prions and CJD. We can weaken the idea that prions cause CJD by showing that prions aren't harmful, or that something else causes CJD.

A. Tempting, but many diseases share the same symptoms. CJD's symptoms cause loss of mental acuity and insomnia. That describes two of the symptoms of the common cold!
Either a disease is CJD or it isn't. To be right, this answer would have had to link the viral infection to patients actually diagnosed with CJD, or with those experiencing a disease so similar that it could also be classed as a neurodegenerative disease.

B. If the therapies cured CJD, then this would be the right answer. But the therapies could be totally ineffective, so the fact that the therapies don't block prion reactions doesn't mean prion reactions aren't the cause of CJD. The mere fact that we use remedies doesn't prove that the remedies work, unfortunately. The therapies might just treat secondary effects or relieve pain.

C. This doesn't show that prions don't cause CJD. This answer just shows that prions cause even more problems. 2

D. The stimulus never mentioned whether malfunctioning prions were hereditary. So this answer tells us nothing about prions.

E. **CORRECT.** Prions aren't bacteria. So if an anti-bacterial drug reverses CJD, then it sounds like bacteria are the cause, not prions. This answer is especially significant since up until now CJD was fatal – we had no way to reverse it (line 45).

Passage 2 - Dunham's Anthropological Dance
Questions 8-14

Paragraph Summaries

1. Dunham's training as a dancer and researcher let her bring dance-isolation to mainstream North American dance.
2. Before Dunham, social scientists neglected dance because they didn't consider it scientific, and because they lacked training in dance.
3. Dunham researched the African origins of Caribbean dance. Against the advice of colleagues, Dunham took part in the dances herself. This let her understand them, and learn the techniques.
4. Dunham created performances using the styles she learned. She managed to include African-American themes in modern dance.

Analysis

In a passage with multiple viewpoints, you should know what each side says, and who the author agrees with.

On one side we have the stodgy, traditional social scientists. Probably, they were white males, though this isn't indicated. The social scientists neglected to study dance (lines 19-23), they advised Katherine Dunham not to dance (lines 33-35), and they couldn't dance (lines 23-25). Losers.

The social scientists had a very formal approach. They thought dance wasn't "scientific", whatever that means. They also thought that an anthropological researcher should stay strictly separated from the people she was studying.

Lines 37-40 shows that the author believes the social scientists were unrealistic in thinking that detachment is good or even possible. The passage also implies that the author agrees with Katherine Dunham's methods, and thinks that Dunham learned valuable things by dancing with those that she studied.

Dunham was a researcher and a dancer. This combination was unique (lines 23-27). As you surely know, dance is a practical skill – it requires training and practice. The author implies that to understand dance, you must be able to do it. Dunham's background in both research and dance thus gave her the ability to study Caribbean dances and their African origins.

I mentioned lines 23-27. They are particularly notable since they suggest that Dunham was the only person trained in both dance and social science – no one else was qualified to study the dances the way that she did.

Paragraphs 1-4 talk about the results of Dunham's work. Her achievements were *very* impressive for a researcher. Normally researchers study things, but they do not *do* things. Dunham did many things. The first paragraph shows that she introduced a completely new technique to North America and Europe. The next time you watch a music video, see if you notice one of the dancers moving one part of their body in isolation. It would seem that's thanks to Dunham!

The final paragraphs show that Dunham was able to create theatre performances that set the stage for the wider inclusion of African-American themes in North American dance.

This isn't in the passage, but Katherine Dunham was African-American herself. She's worth googling, she was as influential as this passage suggests. She even starred in a major Hollywood movie, at a time when it was very rare to feature African-Americans as leads.

You could sum up the main point of the passage as: "Intrepid researcher-dancer defies backwards, traditional ideas about anthropology. She dances with her research subjects, and uses what she learned to make a lasting impression on North American dance."

Question 8

DISCUSSION: The main point is that Dunham had special expertise in dance and anthropology that let her study Caribbean dances. She used what she learned to impact North American dance.

———————————

A. Not necessarily true. Katherine Dunham *defied* anthropology (lines 31-33). It's not clear that she transformed it. Anthropologists eventually recognized that they couldn't stay isolated from their research subjects (line 38), but this might not have been due to Dunham.
B. Not even true. Katherine Dunham was the first to incorporate dance-isolation and African-American themes in North American dance. But there are thousands of traditional cultures in the world – some of these other traditions might have already been used in North American dance.
C. Where did this come from? The passage never mentioned African-American dancers, choreographers, or their aesthetic and political concerns. I don't know how to explain that this is wrong. If you picked this, try to figure out what your thought process was, as the answer is completely unsupported.
D. The passage never says that Dunham discovered the link between Caribbean dances and African dances. It just mentions that there *was* a link (lines 28-31), and that Dunham was interested in studying it.
E. **CORRECT.** This covers the main themes of the passage. Dunham was uniquely suited to study dance (lines 23-27). Paragraphs 1 and 4 show that her studies let her impact modern dance.

Question 9

DISCUSSION: See lines 31-40. Dunham actually danced with the people she was studying. Other anthropologists avoided this, as they thought that they should be neutral observers, and that dance was physically challenging.

The wrong answers simply aren't mentioned in the passage. It's difficult to explain why they're wrong. They're completely unsupported.

If you picked a wrong answer, try to see how you were fooled by the answer choice, and how you could have avoided the error.

———————————

A. The passage never mentions how long various anthropologists studied in the field.
B. The passage actually doesn't mention Dunham's own culture. And it doesn't say whether or not other anthropologists related their research to their own cultures.
C. **CORRECT.** Participative approach = Dunham participated in dances with her research subjects. Lines 31-40 show that Dunham did this and that other anthropologists didn't.
D. The passage never mentioned politics. African-American politics are a common LSAT theme, but that doesn't mean that *every* African-American passage will be political.
E. The passage says that Dunham was familiar with dance, but it doesn't say if Dunham was familiar with Caribbean cultures.

Question 10

DISCUSSION: When a question quotes a specific line, you should read around that line for context. You can answer this question simply be reading the full sentence, which is lines 19-23.

Social scientists valued things that were 'scientifically rigorous'. They avoided studying dance, so presumably they thought that they couldn't study dance with scientific rigor.

The 'peers' are those judging the social scientists' work. If you're a social scientist, your peers will decide if your work is scientifically rigorous and therefore valuable.

———————————

A. Lines 19-23 indicate that social scientists largely ignored dance. So the 'peers' wouldn't have had an opinion on whether dance was interpreted correctly or incorrectly.
B. Lines 19-23 say that social scientists didn't think that research on dance could be scientifically rigorous. Therefore they would probably think that it's *difficult* for social scientists to obtain reliable data, even if those social scientists were well versed in dance traditions.
C. **CORRECT.** This is why social scientists avoided studying dance. They feared that their peers would not think dance could be studied with scientific rigor. See lines 19-23.
D. Lines 26-27 explain why dance experts didn't study dance ethnology. It was because they weren't trained in social science. It had nothing to do with being preoccupied.
E. It's true that social scientists don't think that dance can be studied with rigor. But lines 19-23 don't say *why* rigor was impossible. The passage doesn't say anything about dance forms being too variable.

Question 11

DISCUSSION: Read the whole sentence, lines 23-27. These lines show that Dunham was unique. She had training in both dance and anthropology.

All other experts only had training in social science or dance, but not both. That explains why no one had previously conducted Dunham's studies.

———————————

A. Lines *19-23* explain why social scientists didn't study dance. This question is asking about lines 23-27.
B. This is tempting. But lines 23-27 only talk about why groups are *not* qualified to study dance. This answer has the wrong emphasis: the passage wasn't trying to prove that any group *was* qualified to study dance (apart from Dunham).
C. We're not told why Dunham chose to study dance. Dunham may not have been aware that she was the only dancer qualified to study dance.
D. **CORRECT.** Lines 23-27 show that no dancer had studied dance because they weren't trained in social science research.
E. What? The dancers mentioned in lines 23-27 did not *have* a field of research. That was the point of mentioning them – they were qualified to understand dance, but they weren't researchers.

Question 12

DISCUSSION: In 1935, Dunham began studying the dance forms of the Caribbean. These dances had origins in African dance (lines 28-31).

The passage contradicts all the wrong answers.

_____

A. Lines 10-11 show that both Caribbean and Pacific-island cultures used body isolation. But that's just one technique – we have no idea how similar the two dance cultures were in other respects. Meanwhile, the passage implies that Caribbean dance culture was most similar to *African* dance culture, since Caribbean dance had its origins in African dance.
B. Lines 10-11 mention that Pacific-island dance cultures also used body-isolation. So they might have used these techniques before Caribbean dancers started using them.
C. Lines 45-47 show that Dunham used her Caribbean experience to create *new* forms of ballet.
D. Lines 1-5 show that Dunham was the first to incorporate Caribbean body-isolation techniques into modern American dance.
E. **CORRECT.** Lines 10-11 support this. Caribbean dance culture was influenced by its origins in African dance culture.

This is a fairly straightforward answer, if you get to it. You should always glance over all five answers before spending too much time on any one of them.

Question 13

DISCUSSION: The key points of Dunham's work are the following:

- Expertise in research and in dance
- Immersion in the culture she was studying
- Teaching what she learned to dancers in her own culture.

So you want an answer where someone uses their expertise to immerse themselves in a foreign culture and teach what their learned to their own culture.

The key is participation. None of the wrong answers mentions a researcher participating in what they study.

_____

A. Dunham actually danced the dances she was studying. This answer should have told us the French archaeologist learned to play the instruments she was researching.
B. Same as A. This answer should have said the Australian researcher tried the plants she was researching.
C. This answer says the techniques were used in both countries. Dunham studied techniques that weren't present in her own country.
D. **CORRECT.** Dunham participated in the dances she was studying, and introduced the techniques to America. Here, the teacher actually taught in order to learn the techniques, and he introduced them to Brazil. Everything fits.
E. This answer has no participation. The clothing designer should have actually learned to design foreign clothes himself.

Question 14

DISCUSSION: Read the whole section, lines 31-40. Line 38 is key, the author says that the traditional social scientists' ideas are now "fortunately recognized as unrealistic".

So the author disagrees that anthropologists should remain separate from the people they study, and the author thinks that Dunham was correct to participate in Caribbean dances.

_____

A. The author thinks Dunham made the right decision by participating in dances. So if the social scientists thought that there was a risk of injury, the author wouldn't agree with them.

But it's not even clear that the social scientists did think that there was a risk of injury. Lines 35-36 mention that the dances were physically demanding, but the social scientists actually didn't mention risk of injury per se. The social scientists might simply have considered dancing to be hard work and too much exercise.

B. The social scientists didn't recommend "initial caution". They recommended Dunham avoid dancing altogether!

C. It's true that the author thinks that the researchers were incorrect. But lines 31-40 don't mention scientific rigor. The author never expresses an opinion about the scientific rigor of anthropological research.

D. CORRECT. Line 38 supports this. It's now recognized that anthropological researchers can't remain entirely separate from the people they study.

E. Only lines 19-23 mention scientific rigor. The author never says to what extent they think scientific rigor is possible in the study of dance.

Passage 3 - Happiness Paradox (comparative)
Questions 15-20

<table>
<tr><td>

Paragraph Summaries

</td><td>

Analysis

</td></tr>
<tr><td>

Passage A

1. Happiness paradox. Richer people are happy, richer societies are not happy.
2. Our happiness depends more on the increase in our income than the level of our income. We are not good at understanding this and we over-invest in material goods.
3. Rivalry: A study showed that most people would choose to be poor, but richer than others. East Germans are richer than they used to be. But now they compare themselves to West Germans, so now they feel poorer.

Passage B

1. Does the Solnick-Hemenway study show that we still seek advantages over our rivals via bigger houses?
2. Actually, the data show that richer people feel happier because they're more successful and feel that they have created more value.
3. Two equally successful people will be equally happy, even with different incomes.
4. Wanting to be successful is a noble desire, it means that we want to create value. Fortunately, it also makes us happy.

Note: Paragraph summaries get a bit imprecise on some comparative passages. These two passages have 11 paragraphs between the two of them.

Obviously, I don't keep mental notes on what every single paragraph says. That's only useful for passages with fewer, longer paragraphs (including some comparative passages).

Instead, these notes represent the main points from each passage. They're what I retained from each passage before I moved on to the questions.

</td><td>

One of your most important tasks on a comparative passage is to figure out the main point of each passage, and how the two passages relate to each other. In particular, you should know where the authors agree and where they disagree.

Both authors mentions a study, the Solnick-Hemenway study. Both authors give their *interpretations* of the study.

A study has no objective truth. The Solnick-Hemenway merely reported some observations. Lines 24-33 report the results of the study. The study found that people would prefer to have a smaller amount of money if they were richer than other people.

The author of Passage A thinks that this means we experience rivalry with our peers. We compare ourselves to others, and want to have more money than them.

The author of Passage B has a different interpretation. They say that data shows that we actually care about being successful (lines 50-53). It's true that people with money often feel more successful (lines 55-56), but this is just a correlation. It's the success itself that makes us feel happy (lines 56-57).

Further, we have a noble reason for wanting to feel successful. When we're successful, it's usually because we created value for others. So really we want to feel like we've made contributions to society. (lines 60-66).

So, Passages A and B agree that the study is worthwhile. They disagree on how to interpret the study, and whether rivalry is noble or ignoble.

</td></tr>
</table>

Passage A also talks about habituation – a topic ignored in passage B. Habituation means that we get used to additional income. If you move from $40,000 to $50,000, you will be happy, for a time. But then you'll get used to $50,000. It will feel 'normal'. You'd have been just as happy at $40,000, and you'd probably have had more leisure time.

We're not very good at understanding this. So we keep chasing after money, even though it doesn't make us happier (lines 20-23).

The questions completely ignore the phenomenon of habituation, possibly because only one passage deals with it. This doesn't mean you should ignore something that is only talked about in one passage – that information can give you clues about the author's attitude. Still, a topic is more likely to be useful on comparative passages if it's mentioned in both passages.

Question 15

DISCUSSION: The questions asks about the purpose of both passages. You can answer these questions with 100% certainty. You're looking for something that's mentioned in *both* passages.

Don't just go off of a vague feeling. Check! LSAT students consistently overestimate how much time it takes to refer to the passage. With practice you can learn to find the right lines within 5-10 seconds. This technique lets you be 100% certain that your answer is correct.

You can also eliminate wrong answers by checking the passage. Suppose you know that a concept is mentioned in passage A, but you're not sure if it's in passage B.

You can eliminate the answer by skimming passage B to see if it mentions the concept. Again, this is something you can practice. Have a friend quiz you on whether a passage contains an idea. See how fast you can go.

A. Only passage B mentions value.
B. CORRECT. See lines 1-2 and lines 57-58.
C. Only passage B mentions biology (lines 42-45).
D. Only passage A mentions habituation.
E. Only passage A mentions required income (lines 13-15). Required income relates to habituation, and passage B doesn't mention habituation.

Question 16

DISCUSSION: Several of the wrong answers bring in concepts from passage A in an attempt to confuse you. This should tell you two things:

1. It's very useful to spend extra time reading the passages. If you're 100% clear about what A and B say, then you can easily eliminate wrong answers and save time.
2. If in doubt, check the passage. It doesn't take long, and you can realize that passage B doesn't even talk about most of the things mentioned in the wrong answers.

A. Lines 48-50 show that the author of passage B only mentions genetics in order to disagree with the theory of rivalry. The author never says why we desire to create value – maybe it's a cultural phenomenon.

B. The author never mentions standards of living. This answer is just trying to confuse you with a concept that the author of passage A talked about.

C. **CORRECT.** If you read lines 50-65, it's clear that the author of passage B thinks that success and the feeling of providing value are what make us happy.

   If you win the lottery, that isn't what most people would call success or creating value. So the author of passage B would think that winning the lottery or getting money from luck won't make people happy.

D. This refers to habituation, which was discussed in the first half of passage A. The author of passage B never discusses habituation or small salary increases.

E. The author of passage B never talks about the happiness of society as a whole. But presumably the author would think that society would become happier if the added wealth were due to success. So they wouldn't agree with this answer.

Question 17

DISCUSSION: Line 24 is in passage A. The author thinks that the Solnick-Hemenway study shows we view others as rivals and want to earn more than them.

In lines 41-50, the author of passage B introduces the theory of rivalry, and then completely disagrees with it. The rest of passage B shows that the author thinks that we value success, and that money often accompanies success.

Lines 62-64 show that the author of passage B thinks his opponents are mistaken about human nature. We are not motivated by greed. Instead we crave success because it demonstrates that we have provided value.

Overall, we can say that the author of passage B thinks that passage A's interpretation of the study is wrong in its conclusions, and also unflattering in that it portrays us as greedy and competitive.

A. **CORRECT.** Lines 48-50 show that the author thinks the interpretation is mistaken. Lines 62-64 show that the author thinks that scholars are mistaken about human nature as well. We're motivated not by greed, but to create value.

B. Rivalry is *not* flattering. If the theory of rivalry is true, then it means that we're greedy and we compete with everyone.

C. Lines 62-64 show that the author of passage B thinks that his opponents are mistaken about human nature.

D. Lines 48-50 show that the author of passage B thinks that the conclusions are not valid.

E. This is the complete opposite of what the author of passage B thinks. See lines 41-50 and 62-64.

Question 18

DISCUSSION: Passage A mentions the study in order to introduce the phenomenon of rivalry.

Passage B mentions the study in order to disagree with certain interpretations of it. The author of passage B then introduces their alternate theory: we want to feel successful.

I found the passage B section of these answers harder. I would have said "to present a view that will be argued against".

This shows why you can't get stuck on prephrases. There are multiple ways to say anything. Instead of my version, you can also say: passage B mentions the study in order to introduce the main topic.

Also, the author of passage B technically doesn't disagree with the study. They disagree with certain interpretations of the study. So the study itself isn't introduced as a "view to be argued against".

Meanwhile, passage A doesn't introduce the study as the main topic. Most of passage A is about habituation, which has nothing to do with the study.

———————————

A. The author of passage A uses the study as evidence. It isn't a view to be argued against.
B. Same as A.
C. The first part of this is fine. The second part is wrong. The author of passage B introduced the study along with a view that they *disagreed* with. There was no additional evidence for this view.
D. **CORRECT.** Passage A uses the study as support for their idea: the phenomenon of rivalry. Passage B uses the study as a way of launching into their main topic: the relationships between wealth, success, value and happiness.
E. The first part makes this answer wrong. The main topic of passage A was arguably habituation. The study only introduced the phenomenon of rivalry, which was the smaller part of passage A.
The second half sounds right. Though technically the author of passage A didn't argue against the study itself. But I would have picked this answer if it had had the first half from answer D.

Question 19

DISCUSSION: The question asks what each author would think of a person who wants to be richer than their neighbors.

The author of passage A thinks that such a person is motivated by rivalry.

The author of passage B thinks that such a person is motivated by the desire to feel successful and to feel that they have provided value to others.

———————————

A. Nonsense. Insular means "isolated, withdrawn, like an island". Cosmopolitan means "worldly". Neither word makes sense in context.
B. Arguably, these are reversed. The author of passage A would say that such a person is focussed on themselves, and thus egocentric. The author of passage B would say that such a person wants to provide value to others, and thus is altruistic.
C. Neither author would say how happy such a person is. The question talks about a person who wants to make more money than their neighbors. So we don't know if that person *is* richer than their neighbors or just *wants to* be.
D. **CORRECT.** The word misguided is supported by an overall view of passage A. Lines 20-23 show that we are not good at predicting how extra money will affect our happiness. So someone seeking extra wealth is being silly. The author of passage B thinks that someone who wants to be rich really just wants to help others and provide value (lines 62-66). So wanting to be rich is a good thing.
E. This is completely unsupported. Neither passage mentions luck. Luck is only mentioned in answer C of question 16.
And lines 48-50 show that the author of passage B disagrees with the theory that we are motivated by primeval urges of rivalry.

Question 20

DISCUSSION: As with all questions of this type, you can prove the answer 100% correct by finding references in both passages.

If you're reading this explanation, there's good odds that you chose answer D. But only passage A mentions a paradox. Watch out for this on comparative passages. Passage A does *not* determine what's true in passage B.

You might have hesitated about E because passage A doesn't directly mention data. But passage A cites a study. Everyone would agree that a scientific study is data. That's an example of a warranted term shift.

A. Lines 48-50 show that the author of passage B disagrees with biological origins. Passage A never mentions biology.

B. Neither author does this. I have no idea what this answer refers to – neither passage mentions what popular opinion thinks of the theories discussed. If you picked this, you have some self-examination to do. Ask yourself what gave you the impression this was correct – you'll avoid many errors if you figure out why you chose this.

Note: lines 48-50 show that the theory is commonly heard, but that could just mean several researchers mention it, but not the general public.

C. Same as B. This is completely unsupported. Examine your thought process to see why you found this tempting.

D. Very tempting. Lines 1-2 show that the author of passage A believes that the data represent a paradox. But the author of passage B never mentions a paradox. They seem to think that the situation is perfectly clear: we're motivated by success and value, end of story.

This answer is hard because the early mention of 'paradox' sets the tone for both passages. Remember not to carry ideas from passage A into passage B.

E. CORRECT. The author of passage A cites a study (lines 24-33). That's data.

The author of passage B mentions data directly: see lines 50-53.

Passage 4 - Risk and Voluntariness
Questions 21-27

Paragraph Summaries

1. Policy experts care about how many lives can be saved. Laypeople care about whether a risk is voluntary. But 'voluntary' is ambiguous.
2. Most things are part voluntary and part involuntary. Laypeople mistakenly focus only on the moment an accident occurs, and not what lead up to the accident.
3. "Voluntary" often means "I don't like what that person is doing and I don't want to pay money to help them".
4. The government should simply try to save as many lives as it can. Voluntariness per se should not be a criterion.

Analysis

This is a somewhat complex passage. It's not a good idea to read a passage like this once and move on to the questions. If there are parts you didn't understand, you should go back to reread them. You'll go a lot faster on the questions if you understand the passage. Rereading can save you time.

The passage talks about how the government should improve safety. Most people agree that the government should act to reduce risks.

But normal people and experts disagree. Regular people focus on whether a risk is voluntary. Experts focus on how many lives can be saved for a certain amount of money.

The author agrees with the experts. The central point of the passage is that "voluntary" is not a good way to decide how to reduce risks.

When deciding whether something is voluntary, normal people just focus on the moment in which danger occurs. An airplane passenger is an example. If you're on a plane, you can't move, so the situation feels "involuntary".

But the author points out that people *choose* to go on airplanes. Almost everything is at least partly voluntary (lines 21-25).

The third paragraph says that if we don't like an activity, we'll label it "voluntary" in order to avoid paying for safety improvements. Yet we'll pay to improve the safety of voluntary activities if we like those activities. So we're supportive of protecting firefighters but not skydivers, even though both activities are voluntary.

The final paragraph is a bit cryptic. It says that we should listen to experts and save as many lives as we can – that part is clear.

But what does the second half mean? Departures from the principle should be based on "specific considerations for which voluntariness serves as a proxy". What?

I'll illustrate with an example. Why do people *actually* think fireman deserve to be safe? It's because firemen risk their lives to *protect us*. Skydivers don't protect anyone. Further, people who don't like skydivers think that they risk their lives foolishly.

This distinction causes regular people to say that firefighters deserve support, but sky diving is voluntary.

So the final paragraph suggests that we can make an exception to save firefighters, even if it would be more cost effective to save sky divers. But the exception should be made because fire fighters protect us, not because of voluntariness. "They protect us" is the thing that voluntariness is serving as a "proxy" for, so that's what we should use to justify exceptions.

So the author doesn't think that laypeople are completely wrong. Sometimes their intuitions are valuable. But we should focus on the reasons that make people label something "voluntary". Voluntariness itself is not a useful concept. (lines 50-54)

Most of the wrong answers for these questions are nonsense. When a passage is difficult, the LSAC intentionally writes nonsensical, confusing answers. They assume that you were hallucinating when reading the passage, because most of the wrong answers have nothing to do with anything. There are a few ways to fix this:

1. Reread the passage until you're clear on what it says.
2. Treat the answers as your enemy; assume they're lying.
3. Read all the answers before spending too much time thinking about them. This helps on questions where the right answer is D or E, and is obvious once you reach it.
4. Try to figure out what an answer actually refers to.
5. Justify the answers using actual lines and ideas from the passage. Don't just use your gut.

The most important thing you should know about this passage is that voluntariness is *not* useful. It's a sideshow. See lines 14-19 and 50-54. We should not be using voluntariness for anything.

Question 21

DISCUSSION: This passage is an argument. The main point is that we shouldn't listen to laypeople and their ideas about voluntariness. When we're acting to reduce risks, we should listen to policy experts. Experts say to choose things that save the most lives for the least money.

There are multiple indications that this passage is an argument. Lines 14-19 say that voluntariness is not useful. Paragraphs 2-3 say that voluntariness is vague and arbitrary. Paragraph 4 concludes that we should judge interventions by how many lives they save.

A. This is true, but it's just a fact that supports the main point of the passage. The main point is that we shouldn't consider voluntariness important.
B. **CORRECT.** The final paragraph supports this. The passage is making an argument and the fourth paragraph is the conclusion.
   If you didn't realize that the passage is an argument, look at lines 14-19. The author says that voluntariness is not useful. Paragraphs 2-3 support this assertion, and this in turn leads to the conclusion in paragraph 4.
C. The whole point of the passage is that voluntariness is not a useful concept.
   See lines 14-19, and 50-54. We shouldn't use voluntariness, whether or not experts decide what is voluntary.
D. This isn't even true. The whole point of the passage is that voluntariness is not a useful concept. See lines 14-19 and 50-54.
E. This is true, according to the passage. But it's just a fact that supports the main point. The main point is that therefore voluntariness is not useful for making decisions.

Question 22

DISCUSSION: You're not going to like hearing this, but if you got this question wrong it's because you completely misunderstood the passage.

Lines 12-13 say the right answer. If you found those lines, then this was a very easy question.

All of the wrong answers assume you had no idea what experts believe and what laypeople believe.

This question illustrates why it's extremely important to review a passage if you're not clear on what it says. The wrong answers are designed to trick people who have only a partial understanding of what they read.

A. Lines 34-49 directly contradict this. Laypeople wouldn't support saving skydivers even if there were a good ratio of dollars to lives saved.
B. Experts care about lives saved, not voluntariness. If laypeople deferred to experts, then laypeople wouldn't care about voluntariness.
C. **CORRECT.** Lines 12-13 say this directly.
D. Lines 11-12 say that this is what *experts* focus on.
E. Lines 46-49 say that this is what the author recommends *the government* consider. Total resources available wasn't mentioned as a factor that laypeople consider.

Question 23

DISCUSSION: Lines 33-35 are key. They say that if people don't like something, they will call it "voluntary" and oppose public spending to improve public safety for that activity.

Thus people call skydiving voluntary, and call firefighting involuntary, even though both involve a choice (lines 35-42).

A. Space travel isn't mentioned in the passage.
B. Lines 33-42 indicate that people would call skydiving voluntary in order to avoid spending money to make it safer.
C. I was tempted by this, because people support spending money on firefighters. But line 42 clearly says that firefighting is voluntary. The point of mentioning firefighters was to illustrate that people don't care about voluntariness in a consistent way.
D. **CORRECT.** Lines 25-27 say this directly.
E. Mountain climbing isn't mentioned in the passage.

Question 24

DISCUSSION: For questions like this, there will be a few lines that *directly* support the right answer. If you don't find those lines, you're just guessing. With a small bit of practice you can learn to find lines within 3-5 seconds.

A. Lines 48-50 and 38-39 directly contradict this. The author cares mainly about how many lives we can save.

B. **CORRECT.** Lines 9-13 support this. Voluntariness is a difference between expert judgments and regular judgments. Experts care about lives saved, regular people care whether an activity was voluntary.

C. The passage never says what other risks airline passengers face, apart from crashes.

D. The whole point of the passage is that voluntariness is not a useful concept. The author doesn't care whether or how we decide that something is voluntary.

E. Lines 21-25 touch on this. The author doesn't give an exhaustive opinion on what risks are completely involuntary. They only mention asteroid risks – there could be other involuntary risks as well.

Question 25

DISCUSSION: Read the whole third paragraph and you'll see that the point is that voluntariness is not a useful concept when we're deciding how much money to spend on safety.

So when the author says that voluntariness has "no special magic" he means that it's not a concept we ought to attach any importance to.

I'm unusually insulting about the wrong answer choices below. They make me mad. They're total nonsense designed to trick you. None of them make any sense or refer to anything mentioned in the passage.

A. What? No. By definition, a risk is either voluntary, involuntary, or a bit of both. The two words *do* exhaustively categorize the risks we face. With this answer, the LSAC expected you to be confused about what the word "exhaustively" meant.

B. I think this answer is meant to play on the anti-government paranoia that has long been popular in the United States. The passage doesn't talk about the government "concealing" anything. This is total nonsense.

C. What junk. The author never talked about the meaning of voluntary and involuntary. The point wasn't whether voluntary has a "special meaning". The question is: Is voluntariness a useful concept with which to make decisions?

D. Total rubbish. "Inform people's understanding of the consequences of risk"….what the hell does this refer to? It wasn't in the passage! The phrase I quoted means "how people decide how dangerous an activity is". That simply isn't discussed anywhere.

E. **CORRECT.** Lines 14-19 and 50-54 support this. The point of the passage is that voluntariness is not a useful concept. So when the passage says that there is no special magic to voluntariness, the author means that we shouldn't consider voluntariness as being particularly important.

Question 26

DISCUSSION: As with the other specific detail questions on this passage, you can and should support the right answer using a few lines from the passage.

The wrong answers all refer to concepts out of context. They're intended to trick you, if your understanding of the passage was incomplete.

A. This is very extreme. *Any* activity could involve a loss of human life....even getting out of bed! The author doesn't necessarily think that every activity must be made safer. Especially since we have a limited budget (lines 48-49).
B. **CORRECT.** Lines 21-25 support this. Most risks are voluntary to a certain degree, including environmental risks. Presumably some environmental risks are therefore risky to a greater degree than others.
C. It's true that the author supports policy experts. The author thinks experts are right that we should focus on saving lives.
But the author doesn't think that experts are necessarily any good at judging what is voluntary. The point of the passage is that voluntariness is not important.
D. Lines 48-49 say that we have limited resources. The author did *not* say whether those resources should be increased.
E. Actually, the author spends two paragraphs trashing the beliefs of ordinary people. We ordinary folk focus on voluntariness, but voluntariness is not a useful concept. Nowhere does the author say that it's important to listen to us regular people.

Question 27

DISCUSSION: For author's attitude questions, look for judgments. Authors tend to be quite subtle. Assume that any small positive/negative judgment implies that the author completely agrees/disagrees with a given group.

A. The author didn't say that people misunderstand risk. For instance, lines 35-39 imply that people *do* understand the risks faced by skydivers.
B. It's true that the author doesn't recommend listening to ordinary people. But the author's concern seems to be that regular people don't support *enough* regulation. For instance, the author supports regulating the safety of skydivers (see lines 35-39), whereas ordinary people wouldn't want to spend money improving skydivers' safety.
C. **CORRECT.** Lines 30-35 show two reasons that the author is skeptical of ordinary people's views on voluntariness. Ordinary people only look at part of the situation, and ordinary people decide whether something is voluntary based on whether or not they like the activity.
D. Actually, lines 47-49 show that the author *is* mainly concerned with saving lives.
E. The author *never* criticizes experts. Instead, the author spends paragraphs 2-3 criticizing common people.

Section III - Logic Games
Game 1 - Benefit Concert Bands
Questions 1-7

Setup

This is a linear game, with a few twists. It's not a particularly difficult game. Nonetheless, it's worth noting that all of the game types are becoming less standard.

The LSAC is aware that people are prepping more intensely, so they're reducing the number of games that can be learned from a strategy guide.

To get better at non-standard games, you should repeat them. This way you'll develop an intuition for the underlying patterns on logic games, and you'll be able to handle new, non-standard rules. It's a good idea to repeat the game on your own before reading these explanations.

Now, for the setup. First, you hopefully know that linear diagrams should have a series of horizontal slots:

___ ___ ___ ___ ___ ___
 1   2   3   4   5   6

Next, this game has some pure sequencing rules. These often appear in linear games. Here's the first rule:

V — Z

Here's the second rule:

Z
 ⟍
  ⟋ X
W

The first two rules can and should be combined. Notice that Z is in both rules. You can join both diagrams together using Z:

V — Z
      ⟍
       X
W ⟋

Always watch for multiple rules that mention the same variable.

The third and fourth rules are fairly rare. They say that U must be in the final three spots, and Y must be in the first three.

You *could* just write these in your list of rules, marking something like "U = last 3". Or you could draw a "Not U" symbol under slots 1-3.

I think both of those methods add visual clutter without clarity. I *do* use "not" rules, but not when six of them are required to represent two rules. Instead, here's how I drew these rules:

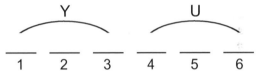

Notice that this diagram is both clear and minimal. Y goes somewhere in the first three and U goes somewhere in the final three.

One glance at the main diagram is enough to remind you of *exactly* what the rules say. I also find this helps me visualize where Y and U can go.

You should always check for deductions before starting. Look for restricted points. The main deduction is that only U or X can go last.

Y must go in the first three spaces, and V, Z and W must go before X. So only U or X are left to go sixth. You *could* draw this on the diagram:

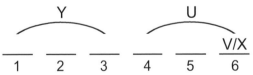

However, I would only do this if you're prone to forgetting this type of deduction. If you're an advanced student of logic games, this type of deduction is likely second nature to you.

It might be worth adding Y – X on your ordering diagram. X has three variables before it, so X can't go in the first three spaces. However, I haven't drawn this on mine, as it's easy for me to see this.

Main Diagram

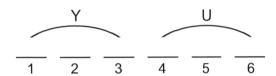

Notice that all six variables are represented, along with their rules. This setup makes it pointless to draw a separate list of the variables (UVWXYZ). Such a list adds no value, and wastes space and time.

This setup also makes it easy to visualize possibilities. You don't have to hold any rules in your head.

It's difficult to explain what you see inside your own head. But when I look at these, I can see V – Z – X floating over the diagram and interacting with Y and U.

Obviously, whether or not you can do this depends on your visualization skills. But I expect it's a learnable skill to some extent. Practice seeing the variables move around over the diagram: it really comes in handy for sequencing games.

Question 1

Unusually, this question is not an 'acceptable order' question. Usually first questions are. If the first question is *not* an acceptable order question, it's a sure sign that you were expected to make a deduction in the setup.

Here, the only deduction is that you can combine rules 1 and 2 to get this diagram:

V – Z
   ⟩ X
 W

Since it's the only deduction, this diagram is almost certainly what will let us get the right answer. We're looking for something that can't go fifth. That means something that has more than two other variables after it.

That's V. Both Z and X have to go after V, so V can go fourth at latest.

B is CORRECT.

44

Question 2

When a question gives you a new rule, you can combine it with the existing rules to make a deduction.

We know Z is after V and before X:

V — Z
‾‾‾‾‾‾ X
  W ⟋

This question also places Z before Y. And we know Y can go third at latest.

So Z is after V, and before Y. That's three variables. Since Y can't go later than third, we must place these three variables in slots 1-3:

```
                    U
               ⌒‾‾‾‾‾⌒
  V     Z     Y    ___   ___   ___
 ‾‾‾   ‾‾‾   ‾‾‾   ‾‾‾   ‾‾‾   ‾‾‾
  1     2     3     4     5     6
```

The question asks about the earliest we can place W. Let's first look at the remaining variables. W comes before X. U is the only variable left, and the only rule for U is that it goes somewhere 4-6. Here's how I draw this:

```
                  W — X , U
  V     Z     Y    ___   ___   ___
 ‾‾‾   ‾‾‾   ‾‾‾   ‾‾‾   ‾‾‾   ‾‾‾
  1     2     3     4     5     6
```

The line between W – X shows that W comes somewhere before X. The comma between W – X and U means that there are no rules governing where you can place U. It could go before W – X, in between them, or after them.

This way of drawing "W – X, U" is a flexible method of visualizing everything that can be true, without clutter.

There is no reason we can't place W fourth, so **C** is **CORRECT.**

Question 3

This question tests your ability to apply the ordering rules. Let's look at them again:

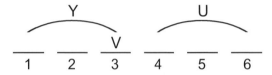

The question places V third:

```
        Y                   U
     ⌒‾‾‾⌒             ⌒‾‾‾‾‾⌒
  ___   ___   V     ___   ___   ___
 ‾‾‾   ‾‾‾   ‾‾‾   ‾‾‾   ‾‾‾   ‾‾‾
  1     2     3     4     5     6
```

We know that Y has to go in slots 1-2. Who else can go there?

Not U. They must go 4-6.
Not Z. They must go after V
Not X. They must go after Z.

So only W can also go in slots 1-2. We get this diagram:

```
    Y , W              Z — X , U
  ___   ___   V     ___   ___   ___
 ‾‾‾   ‾‾‾   ‾‾‾   ‾‾‾   ‾‾‾   ‾‾‾
  1     2     3     4     5     6
```

The commas indicate that variables are interchangeable, while the line between Z – X indicates that there's an ordering rule for them to obey.

You might have seen Powerscore draw Y and W like this: Y/W   W/Y

That works too. However, that method doesn't work well for slots 4-6, which is why I prefer my more flexible method. You get a very clear view of where every variable can go.

B is CORRECT. W has to be 1st or 2nd, so they are always before Z in this scenario.

A, C and **E** are wrong because U could be before Z – X, in between them, or after them.

D is wrong because Y and W are interchangeable in this scenario.

Question 4

For this question, ZW are a block. Let's look at what other rules apply. We know that X is after ZW, and V is before ZW:

V—[ZW]—X

This is not an easy group of variables to place. In fact, ZW can *only* go third and fourth.

You may be thinking "how can you *know* that"? If so, I encourage you *not* to think. Instead, draw.

Make a diagram with ZW second and third. Doesn't work: V has to go first, and there's no space to put Y in 1-3.

Make a diagram with ZW fourth and fifth. Doesn't work, X has to go last, and there's no space to put U in 4-6.

I'm sure you can see why we can't put ZQ in 1-2 or 5-6. It's because V has to go before them, and X has to go after.

So with two diagrams, you can prove that this is the only possible setup:

With practice, you can draw 2-3 test diagrams in about 15 seconds. If you find it slow going, it's because you haven't practiced, and because you don't have the rules memorized. But you can learn to be faster.

I don't "think" about most logic games. I just try stuff, and then I "see" what works and what doesn't. Logic games are a very mechanical process. Usually the new rules for individual questions are quite restrictive.

Anyway, **E** is **CORRECT**. Z has to go in slot 3.

A and **C** are wrong because U and X are interchangeable in this scenario.

B and **D** are wrong because V and Y are interchangeable in this scenario. Either one could be first or second.

Question 5

It can be helpful to identify the groups that *can't* perform first.

U can't perform first, because they must go 4-6.

Z can't perform first, because they come after V.

X can't perform first, because Z, V and W come before X.

That leaves V, Y and W. They have no variables in front of them, so they all could go first.

D is **CORRECT.**

Question 6

This question places W immediately before X. That rearranges the ordering rules:

$$V - Z - \boxed{WX}$$

Nobody but U can go after X. So in this question, WX and U fill the final three spots:

$$V - Z , Y \quad \Big| \quad \boxed{WX} , U$$

$$\underline{\quad} \quad \underline{\quad} \quad \underline{\quad} \quad \underline{\quad} \quad \underline{\quad} \quad \underline{\quad}$$
$$1 \qquad 2 \qquad 3 \qquad 4 \qquad 5 \qquad 6$$

I put a dividing line in the middle to make clear which side the floating variables go on. Though on my own sheet I just drew the blocks a bit further apart. I find these floating variables the easiest way to visualize who can go where. No need to draw five separate scenarios – this one diagrams lets you see them all in your head.

A doesn't work because U can only go before WX or after, so U can only be fourth or sixth.

B doesn't work because V is before Z. Since Z is third at the latest in this scenario, V can only go first or second.

C doesn't work because W has to go in the final three slots in this scenario.

D is **CORRECT.** This diagram proves it:

$$\boxed{WX} , U$$

$$\overset{V}{\underline{\quad}} \quad \overset{Z}{\underline{\quad}} \quad \overset{Y}{\underline{\quad}} \quad \underline{\quad} \quad \underline{\quad} \quad \underline{\quad}$$
$$1 \qquad 2 \qquad 3 \qquad 4 \qquad 5 \qquad 6$$

I filled in only the first half in order to emphasize how you should view these diagrams. This is a "could be true" question, so you just have to show that an ordering is possible.

You don't have to prove everything, or even finish the scenario, since you know that any order for 4-6 is legal as long as it fits the constraints we set up for this question. WXU or UWX are both fine.

E is wrong because Z has to go in slots 1-3 for this question.

Question 7

If you're like most LSAT students, I'll bet you *hate* rule substitution questions. If I told you they don't have to be hard, would you believe me?

The trick is to look at the full effect of a rule, and describe it another way. Let's look at what we know about X:

V – Z
      ⟍
        ⟍ X
      ⟋
  W ⟋

X comes after Z, V and W. X also comes after Y, because Y has to be in one of the first three places, and X already has three people in front.

So Z, V, W and Y comes before X. Only U *could* come after X. That's the full extent of the rule.

And now that's we've looked at the full extent of the rule, it's obvious that **A** is **CORRECT.**

You can also answer these questions by elimination. An answer is wrong if it allows something that shouldn't be allowed, or if it prevents something that normally would be allowed.

B is wrong because it puts V before W. Normally, it's possible for W to go before V.

C is wrong because it leaves out Z. With the rule in this answer, it would be possible for Z to go after X.

D is wrong because it allows Z to go after X. For example, this order is normally illegal, but it would be allowed with this rule:

V	W	Y	U	X	Z
1	2	3	4	5	6

That diagram also proves that **E** wrong. E allows Z to be after X as long as X is in five. That is different from the normal rules.

Game 2 - Research Team
Questions 8-12

Setup

This is an in-out grouping game. If you found this game hard, you're not alone. Most students find that in-out grouping games are one of the hardest game types on the LSAT.

But I've got good news for you: this is also one of the most common and standard types of games on the LSAT. That might not seem like good news, but it means you can practice many games of this type.

You'll find that once they practice this type of game, it becomes one of the *easiest* game types. So if you work at it, you can turn in-out games from a disadvantage to an advantage.

I'll note that if you look at games classifications online, they lump a bunch of different games together as "in-out grouping games". The type I'm referring to here has the following characteristics:

1. All of the rules are conditional statements.
2. All of the rules can be connected together to form one big diagram and its contrapositive.

Now, since all the rules can be combined, it is *not* sensible to draw them separately. It's better to just start combining them right off the bat.

Some students don't agree, at first. They worry and fret and feel they can't do it. Instead, they draw all the rules separately, and the contrapositives, and end up with a jumble of rules. They then spend 3-4 minutes looking for deductions, but their drawing is so confusing that they never make a single one. I've never seen a student make proper deductions when they start by drawing the rules separately.

Don't be like that. You *can* do this. Just follow along, and draw the diagram for yourself on paper. Do it a few times and it will feel like second nature.

The key to combining rules is to look for multiple rules that mention the same variable. You can always connect two rules if they have a variable in common. You might have to take the contrapositive of one of them, if the common variable is in the form "M" and "Not M" (i.e. negated) form.

Enough preamble, let's look at the first rule:

This means that if M is in, both O and P are out. Don't ever forget the + and 'or' signs in between arrows. They're very important.

The next rule looks like this:

It may not be obvious how this connects, but both rules mention P. So let's take the contrapositive of rule 2:

To take the contrapositive, you reverse the terms, and negate them. You also change "and" to "or" and vice-versa.

Now both the first and second rule have a "not P". We can connect the two rules like this:

It's a mistake to move on to the third rule if you don't first combine the first rules like we just did.

The third rule mentions M, and M is already on the diagram, so you can connect the third rule like this:

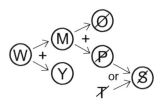

That's it! That one big diagram covers all the rules.

Learning how to draw it is one thing. You also need to know how to read it. You must read these diagrams left to right.

As an example: if W is in, then both Y and M must be in as well. Since M is in, O and P and S are out. We don't know anything about T, it could be in or out. I've circled what we know, *if* W is in:

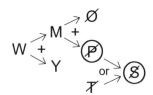

Let's look at another example. What happens if P is out? We only know one thing: S is also out:

We don't know anything about the other variables. Maybe M is in, or maybe it is out. P being out is just a *necessary* condition for M being out, so it doesn't tell us anything about M.

The more you do these games, the more this type of diagram will make sense. It's like learning a language, you can't read them fluently at first. But once you *can* read this diagram, it's by far the most powerful way to solve these games.

Now, we also need to take the contrapositive of the main diagram. You do this just like you'd take any other contrapositive:

1. Reverse the order
2. Negate everything
3. Change 'and' to 'or', and vice versa.

Here it is:

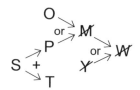

I *highly* recommend you draw this yourself on paper and practice the three steps. Taking contrapositives is a very mechanical process, which means it gets easy with practice.

There is one other rule that doesn't fit on this diagram. At least four variables are selected. There could be more than four selected as well of course – four is just the minimum.

This rule was in the opening paragraph – you should always scan the opening paragraph to see if there's any rules hidden in there.

Lastly, there are no rules for Z. A good way to represent this is to draw Z with a circle around it. I drew this near my other two diagrams.

Main Diagram

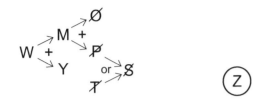

At least four employees are selected.

Question 8

For acceptable order questions, go through the rules and use them to eliminate answers one by one.

I do not recommend using your diagram to solve acceptable order questions, even on in-out grouping games. It's faster to use the rules, and reading them again helps you to memorize them.

Rule 1 eliminates **A.** M and P can't go together.

Rule 2 eliminates **C** and **D.** If S is on a team, then both T and P must be there.

Rule 3 eliminates **E.** If W is on a team, then M must also be on that team.

B is **CORRECT.** It violates no rules.

Question 9

This is a common question type on in-out games. It asks which two people can't go together.

You're looking for the following relationship:

1. The variable on the left is in positive form. i.e. "S"
2. The variable on the right is in negative form i.e. "M̶"
3. **Example:** S → M̶, M → S̶

In other words, one variable being *in* forces the second variable *out*. This method works whether you look at the main diagram or the contrapositive. Pick a pair of variables from an answer and look for the left most variable on either of the diagrams. Then see if it matches the form I described above.

A is wrong. There are no arrows connecting M and T.

B is wrong. There are no arrows connecting O and Y.

C is wrong. Z has no rules, it can never force another variable out.

D is **CORRECT.** If S is in, W is out:

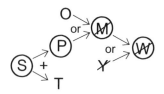

(T is in too of course. I've only circled the variables leading from S to W in order to clarify the relationship you're looking for on this question.)

E is wrong. If W is in, Y is in. Clearly, those two can be together.

Question 10

I found this question hard. I eventually figured out what I was missing: I had forgotten that at least four employees must be selected.

This question places Y out. That also forces W out. You can draw this as an in-out diagram, it may help you to keep track:

I	O
—	Y
—	W
—	
—	

We need at least four variables in. I've drawn that as a reminder in this diagram, but I won't always repeat it.

So, Y and W are out. Since we need at least four employees in, we can have, at most, two more employees in the out group.

The answers ask who *can't* be placed in. The right answer will be an employee that forces more than two other employees out if they are in.

That's M. Refer to the diagram, look at "M in", and you'll see that O, P and S must be out. That's five people out total, which is too many:

I	O
	Y
	W
	O
	P
	S

E is **CORRECT.**

This listing shows that all the others could be in together:

I	O
T	Y
Z	W
P	M
O	
S	

This scenario is actually just the contrapositive of the main diagram:

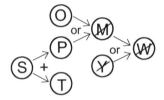

(I added Z in the in/out diagram above too, since Z can always be in)

Question 11

Another tricky question. I found trial and error to be the most effective method. If P is out, then S is out.

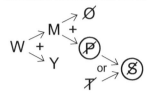

Only a max of four employees can be out. So we've only got two employees left to place out, at most.

All of the wrong answers force three people out, which makes a total of five out. That's one too many.

A places M and O out. M out means W is out, for a total of five out: P, S, M, O, W

B places M and T out. M out means W is out, for a total of five out: P, S, M, T, W

C places M and Z out. If M is out, then W is also out. That makes a total of five out: P, S, M, Z, W

D is **CORRECT.** This answer places O and T out. O being out doesn't force anyone out.

T being out only forces S out, and S was already out on this question. Here's the in-out diagram for this that shows this answer works:

I	O
Y	P
Z	S
W	O
M	T

In fact, this answer is just the main diagram, plus Z. So it obeys all the rules:

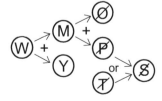

E places O and Y out. If Y is out, then W also has to go out. That makes a total of five out: P, S, O, Y, W

53

Question 12

This is a slightly unusual question. *Normally,* when looking for a pair where at least one has to be in, you would look for a pair with the sufficient negated, and the necessary in. E.g. $Q \rightarrow M$

But there are no pairs like that in this game. So we'll have to use a different method to find out what variables must be in.

The fast way to solve this question is to find a couple of working orders. If you find an order that works, you can use it to eliminate wrong answers. Any variables not included in your working order obviously don't *have* to be in.

To quickly make two working scenarios, I used the main diagrams. I just started from the left and fulfilled all the sufficient conditions. Like this:

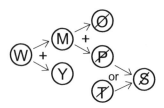

For the first diagram, that gives us WYM in, and OPST out. Add Z in to make four variables in.

Let's make another working scenario, using the second diagram. If you activate all the sufficient conditions, SPTO are in, and MYW are out.

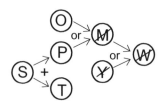

I also left Z out, because this question is asking who *has* to be in. Z doesn't have to be in if we already have four variables in.

So now we have two groups of employees that fulfill all the rules:

WYMZ   and   SPTO

You can use these groups to eliminate answers.

A is wrong. The first group doesn't include O or S.

C is wrong. The first group doesn't include P and S.

E is wrong. The second group doesn't include Y or Z.

Hopefully this method makes sense. I'm attempting to describe the kind of short cut that high scorers use routinely.

Under timed conditions, it took me all of 10 seconds to create those two groups. It takes longer to explain it, because I'm walking you through the steps I went through instantaneously in my head. I recommend practicing this question a few times to get better at quickly creating scenarios to disprove answers.

So now we've narrowed things down to **B** and **D.** If you use a quick method to eliminate three answers, you can afford to spend more time testing the remaining two. Let's see if we can create a scenario without OW or without TY.

This scenario eliminates **B.** MYZT. It obeys all the rules, and doesn't include O or W. For purposes of illustration, I'll highlight all the variables I selected across both diagrams. MYTZ are in, POSW are out.

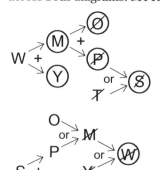

You must read the diagrams left to right. We've covered all seven variables across both diagrams, and none of the rules conflict.

D is **CORRECT.** It's impossible to construct a correct scenario without either T or Y.

54

Game 3 - Repertory Theatre
Questions 13-18

Setup

This game is a mixture of linear and grouping. I don't classify games beyond that. Few people who score well on logic games really care about games classifications. That's just something prep companies invent to sell books and courses, and also because they enjoy classifying things.

It's more important to repeat games and develop an intuitive sense of how to draw the rules.

Ok, let's look at the setup of this game. First, you need to think about how to draw this game. There are three groups, and three time slots. The first question is a good guide to how to represent this. They've arranged the groups vertically, and the times left to right. I've added a slight modification to make clear that 8 o'clock is after 7 o'clock.

```
1  __    __

2  __    __

3      __
   7   8   9
```

I'm just going to draw the diagram like this once, so that it's perfectly clear to you where 123 and 789 are. But for future diagrams, I'm going to leave off the 789, like this:

```
1  __    __

2  __    __

3      __
```

The 789 diagram is very cluttered. If you put too much stuff on your diagrams, your brain won't be able to make sense of them.

And actually, my own diagrams are even more minimal. My main diagram has the 123, but my diagrams for individual questions generally don't have numbers. Here's a scenario from question 17, drawn the same way I'd draw it on my page:

```
W      S
__     __


__     __

       R
       __
```

It's lightning fast to draw a diagram like that, and by glancing at the main diagram I can orient myself easily. My main diagram is on the second page, beside the questions.

Even looking at this, without checking my main diagram, I find it obvious to see which groups are 123 and 789.

However, I'll be including the 123 for the rest of the explanations, for clarity. However, I encourage you to experiment with the most minimal diagrams that make sense to you.

I've just given you a little peek behind the curtain. The explanations in all of my books are very similar to what I would draw on test day, but they're not identical.

This is true of *every* set of logic games diagrams you might find online. LSAT instructors need to add some complexity in order to make diagrams clear for explanatory purposes. But you should leave off any details you don't find essential. Your diagrams only have to make sense to you.

Ok, now, for the rules. I'll start with rules 1 and 4, as they can't be drawn on the diagram. Rule 1 says that W is before H:

W–H

You could also add this rule to the diagram as "not" rules, where you draw "not H" under slot 7, and "not W" under slot 9. I'm avoiding this, because that's a tactic for beginning students. Advanced students can tell just by looking at W – H that H can't go at 7 o'clock and W can't go at 9 o'clock.

Rule 4 says that H and M don't go in the same group:

You may recognize this as a diagram that's also used in linear games. I've never run into a problem using it for both linear and grouping games.

If this were a linear rule, it would mean that HM can't go beside each other, in either order. As a grouping rule, it means that H and M can't be in the same group.

Rules 2 and 3 can be drawn directly on the diagram. I put them as 'not' rules to the right of each group. R can't go in group 2 and S can't go in group 3:

1 ___   ___

2 ___   ___ R̸

3   ___   S̸

Main Diagram

1 ___   ___

2 ___   ___ R̸

3   ___   S̸

① W–H

② [HM̸]

56

Question 13

For acceptable order questions, go through the rules and use them to eliminate answers one by one.

Rule 1 eliminates **B.** The western is supposed to begin earlier than the horror film.

Rule 2 eliminates **D.** The sci-fi film can't be shown on screen three.

Rule 3 eliminates **E.** The romance can't be shown on screen two.

Rule 4 eliminates **C.** The horror and mystery films must be shown on different screens.

A is **CORRECT.** It violates no rules.

Question 14

This is another type of acceptable order question. Remember that the two movies in the answers are on screen two. They are shown at 7 and 9.

It's best to go through the rules one at a time to see if a rule proves an answer correct.

The first rule proves that **C** is **CORRECT.** The western must go before the horror film. That means that W can't go at 9.

You should, of course, check that none of the answers violate rules 2-4. And all the other answers are fine.

I'm not going to bother proving that the other answers work. It's not something you'd ever want to do under timed conditions.

If you think that one of the other answers also doesn't work, then you're misreading the rules. I don't know which rule you're misreading, so I can't solve the problem except by telling you to read the rules again and find your mistake.

Question 15

I actually got this question wrong when I took the test under timed conditions. (Yes, I make mistakes)

I chose **A,** because I forgot that the romance film can't go in group 2.

But I'm getting ahead of myself, I'll show you the diagram we can draw based on the new rule this question gives us.

This question says that W and S are in the same group. That means they're in group 1 or 2, because only those groups have two spaces.

We can also figure out the order of W and S. The western has to go before the horror film, so the western can't go in group 3. Therefore the western goes at 7, and the sci-fi goes at 9.

So we get these two diagrams:

```
1 W         S
  ___       ___

2           ___ R̶
  ___

3           S̶
      ___
```

```
------------------------------------------

1 ___       ___

2 W         S   R̶
  ___       ___

3           S̶
      ___
```

But actually, the first diagram won't work. The romance film can't go in group two, so it would have to fill group three.

That would leave the mystery and horror films to go in group 2. And that violates rule 4.

So we're working from the second diagram. One of M/H goes in group 3, because they can't go together:

```
     R, M/H
1  ___       ___

2  W         S   R̶
   ___           

3    M/H       S̶
   ___
```

The romance film and the other one of M/H fill group 1. Just remember that the horror film can't go at 7 o'clock, because it comes after the western.

This is a could be true question.

A can't be true. The second screen is filled by the western and the sci-fi film.

B is **CORRECT.** This diagram shows that it works:

```
1 R         M
  ___       ___

2 W         S   R̶
  ___           

3   H         S̶
  ___
```

C doesn't work. If the romance film is on screen three, then the mystery film and the horror film would have to go together, which violates rule 4.

D can't be true. If the sci-fi film starts at 7, then the western would start at 9, since they're in the same group. But the western can't start at 9 – it has to go before the horror film (rule 1).

E doesn't work. This question says that the western is on the same screen as the sci-fi film. Only screens 1 and 2 have two spaces, and neither of them have a show starting at 9 o'clock.

58

Question 16

This question places the romance before the western. We also know that the western is before the horror film. So we get this order:

R – W – H

That means the romance is at 7 o'clock, the western is at 8 o'clock, and the horror film is at 9 o'clock.

The romance film can't go in group 2, so it must be in group 1. The western is in group 3, as that's the only screen with an 8 o'clock showing:

1 R   ___

2 ___   R̸

3   W   H̸

Next, the mystery and horror films must be in different groups (rule 4). That means one of them is in group 1, and the other in group 2:

1 R   M/H

2 ___   ___ S, H/M

3   W

The sci-fi film also has to go in group 2, as it's the only group left open. **E is CORRECT.**

In case you were wondering, I drew S and M/H to the right of group two, with a comma, to indicate that they both go in that group, in either order.

Question 17

This question appears similar to question 14. It looks like a rule based "acceptable order" question.

Unfortunately, I went through every rule and none of them seemed to directly eliminate any answers.

When you're stuck, you should consider the most restricted variables. In this game, the horror film and the mystery film are quite restricted, as rule 4 says they can't go together.

Notice that answers **A-D** all include one of the horror and mystery films. So they automatically fulfill our toughest rule.

E does not have either the horror or the mystery film, so let's start there.

The western and the sci-fi film fill group one, and one of H/M fill group 3:

1 W   S

2 ___   ___ R, H/M

3   H/M

So the romance film and the other H/M go in group 2. But this doesn't work: rule 3 says that the romance film can't go in group 2.

E is CORRECT.

This is a hard question, but it fits a pattern. If a question seems impossible, look for what's *not* included in the answer choices. The LSAC knows that people aren't very good at imagining things that aren't listed, so they're pretty predictable at using this trick to make hard questions.

Question 18

This question places sci-fi and romance on the same screen. Rule two says that the sci-fi film can't go on screen 3. Rule three says that the romance film can't go on screen 2.

So if the sci-fi and romance film are together, they have to be shown on screen 1, in either order:

1 S/R   R/S

2 ___   ___ R̶

3   ___ S̶

We have the western, the horror film, and the mystery left to place. We know the horror and the mystery have to fill two groups, so one of H/M fills group 3:

1 S/R   R/S

2 ___   ___ R̶

3   H/M   S̶

The western and the other H/M goes in group 2. The western has to go in 7 o'clock, because rule 1 says the western is before the horror film:

1 S/R   R/S

2 W   M/H R̶

3 H/M   S̶

A is **CORRECT.** The western must start at 7 o'clock.

B-E all could be true, but don't have to be. R/S and H/M are interchangeable for this question.

Game 4 - Lectures on Birds
Questions 19-23

Setup

This is a linear game, with each lecture assigned to one hall.

It's best to keep your diagrams as simple as possible, so I draw the lectures above the slots, and the halls underneath the slots. I'll demonstrate by drawing the main diagram with the first and second rules:

$$\underset{G}{\rule{1cm}{0.4pt}} \quad \underset{}{\rule{1cm}{0.4pt}} \quad \underset{}{\rule{1cm}{0.4pt}} \quad \underset{H}{\rule{1cm}{0.4pt}} \quad \underset{}{\rule{1cm}{0.4pt}}$$

Notice that I haven't included numbers. If you make diagrams without numbers, you'll very quickly learn to see which slot is which. You'll also be able to draw diagrams much faster, with less space.

I usually include numbers in my diagrams for explanatory purposes, but with only five slots it's better to show you how I would *actually* draw this.

There's not much we can do with the third rule. It says that three of the lectures are in Gladwyn hall. It's best just to memorize rules like this, though it's not a bad idea to include a note in your list of rules, like so:

3 G

The most important thing you must realize about the first rule is that if there are three Gs, then there are only two Hs.

This comes up over and over, so I'll repeat it: **there are only two Hs.**

The next two rules also can't be drawn on the diagram. The fourth rule says that S is in Howard Auditorium, and that S is before O:

$$\underset{H}{\underline{S}} \quad \underline{\quad} \quad \underline{O}$$

Once again, this diagram includes as much detail as necessary, but no more.

The fifth rule is similar. T is before P, and P takes place in Gladwyn Hall:

$$\underline{T} \quad \underline{\quad} \quad \underset{G}{\underline{P}}$$

That's it. As with most modern logic games, there's no way to combine these rules to draw deductions. The most important things on modern logic games are making a clear representation of the rules, and memorizing the rules.

Is it possible to make a couple of scenarios. We know that there are only two Hs, and S has to take place in H.

S is also in front of O. So either S can go fourth, or S can go in one of 2/3.

If S is fourth, we know that O is last:

$$\underset{G}{\rule{1cm}{0.4pt}} \quad \underline{\quad} \quad \underline{\quad} \quad \underset{H}{\underline{S}} \quad \underline{O}$$

If S is 2/3, then the placement of G and H is completely determined, because we've placed both Hs:

$$\underset{G}{\rule{1cm}{0.4pt}} \quad \underset{G}{\overset{\frown}{\rule{1cm}{0.4pt}}} \quad \underset{H}{\underset{S}{\rule{1cm}{0.4pt}}} \quad \underset{H}{\rule{1cm}{0.4pt}} \quad \underset{G}{\overset{O}{\rule{1cm}{0.4pt}}}$$

O is floating to the right of S in the second diagram. This is a way of placing the fourth rule directly on the diagram: O is after S. That way it's harder to forget the rule.

The line above the second and third slots indicates that S could go second or third (you have to move H too).

There are no added deductions you can make by placing S 2nd or 3rd, so I represented both possibilities as one scenario. The two positions are interchangeable.

61

The scenarios on the previous page are very rough diagrams. They are useful because they let you see how limited the game is. S can only go second, third or fourth.

I find that when I make these diagrams in advance, I see things that I wouldn't have noticed otherwise. Many questions become very obvious, as I've realized the possibilities are quite limited.

I encourage you to sketch out a couple of scenarios before you start games. You may be surprised at the insights you gather. Try to split the scenarios based on an objective factor, such as "S is fourth, or S is 2/3". Don't just draw randomly.

I normally only draw scenarios when I can make a clear division between two exclusive possibilities. i.e. Things can only go one way, or another way.

Main Diagram

G   —   —   H   —

(1)   3 G

(2)   S / H   —   O

(3)   T   —   P / G

Two scenarios

S fourth

—   —   —   S / H   O
G

S second or third

—   —   S   —   O
G   G   H   H   G

Question 19

For acceptable order questions, go through the rules and use them to eliminate answers one by one.

On this question, you must combine two rules to eliminate **D** and **C**. That's unusual, but the process is the same.

When I solved this, I eliminated all the answers I could get rid of with a single rule, then I examined the remaining answers in more detail to see if they violated a combination of rules.

Rule 5 eliminates **A** and **B.** Petrels must be lectured on earlier than Terns.

None of the other rules eliminate any answers on their own.

Rules 1 and 4 eliminate **D.** The first lecture is in Gladwyn Hall, and the Sandpipers lecture is in Howard Auditorium. So Sandpipers can't go first.

Rules 2 and 5 eliminates **C.** Petrels must go in Gladwyn Hall, and the fourth lecture must be in Howard Auditorium. This answer places P fourth.

E is **CORRECT.** It violates no rules.

Question 20

Open-ended "must be false" and "must be true" questions can be among the hardest logic games questions.

Sometimes you have a flash of insight and you can get the answer right away. Other times you have no choice but to try every answer, using trial and error.

I"m going to try to help you get that flash of insight. The key is to look at the answers and see what rules they relate to. Here the answers place G and H. Let's see what rules relate to G and H:

- There are three Gs. Therefore there are two Hs.
- A G is first
- An H is fourth.

The right answer will violate one of these rules. None of the answers violate the rules about putting G first or H fourth. So the right answer almost certainly violates the first rule: there are three Gs and two Hs.

Let's look at the answers that mention H, because H is the more restricted variable. One of the two Hs is already fourth, thanks to rule two. So only one of the other lectures can take place in H.

B puts H in second and third. We also know H is fourth. That's three Hs, which is too many, so **B** is **CORRECT.**

D places two Hs, but one of them is fourth. Since there was already an H fourth, this answer only requires two Hs total. So **D** is possible.

There's basically no way for **A, C** or **E** to violate a rule. Three lectures take place at G, so there's no way for an answer to place too many Gs.

I hope this helps you see that there's usually a *method* that you can apply to quickly solve "must be false" questions. The right answer was simply based on combining two rules: rule 2 and rule 3.

Question 21

When a question gives you a new rule, there is always a way to combine that rule with one of the existing rules. To do this effectively, you should have the regular rules memorized.

When you have all the rules in your head, it's *much* easier to combine them.

This question says that terns are lectured on in H. Here are the existing rules that relate to that:

- Sandpipers are lectured on in H (rule 4).
- Only two lectures are H (rule 3).
- One of the H lectures is fourth (rule 2).

Whew, there are quite a few involved in this question. Let's go through step by step.

There are two Hs. For this question, S and T are the lectures that take place in H.

Since one of the Hs is fourth, that means that one of S and T will be fourth. Whenever there are only two possibilities, you can split things up into two scenarios. Separate scenarios will let you get more deductions:

			S	
G			H	

			T	
G			H	

This may seem a lengthy process when I explain it. But it actually takes longer to explain than to draw. Success at logic games comes from experience. A skilled student of logic games can get the two scenarios above with 5-10 seconds of drawing and deductions.

Likewise, a skilled student will make all the deductions I'm about to walk you through, and they'll make them very quickly. If you move on without understanding this question intuitively, then you won't learn that skill. Keep practicing questions like this until they're second nature. Draw the diagrams on your own, too.

Ok, so we made two scenarios, with T and S fourth. Other rules mention those birds. T is before P, and S is before O. (rules 4 and 5)

			S	O
G			H	G

			T	P
G			H	G

In both cases, the fifth lecture takes place in Gladwyn Hall. This is because on this question, S and T are the lectures that take place in Howard Auditorium. (Also, rule 5 says that P takes place in Gladwyn Hall)

Ok, so now we have to place T in the first diagram, and S in the second. S and T both take place in H, so they can't go first. And they both have something after them, so they can't go third. Therefore they each go second:

	T	P	S	O
G	H	G	H	G

	S	O	T	P
G	H	G	H	G

The next step would be placing R first in both diagrams. I left that off to make the previous step easier to follow.

A is **CORRECT.** In the second diagram, O is third and is in Gladwyn Hall.

These dual scenario deductions are a very common pattern for some "could be true" and "must be true" questions. The question can be split into two scenarios. When you fill them both out, you'll then see what can be true in both diagrams, and what must be true in both.

As I said, you can get quite fast at this with practice. The alternative is trial and error. That can be a perfectly acceptable method. You can get lucky, try A, and see that it's the right answer. But the problem with trial and error is that you don't usually know where to start, and you may have to try every answer.

Question 22

The diagrams from question 21 let us solve this question. **A** is **CORRECT**. O can be fifth, and in Gladwyn Hall.

Here's the diagram that proves it:

$$\frac{R}{G} \quad \frac{T}{H} \quad \frac{P}{G} \quad \frac{S}{H} \quad \frac{O}{G}$$

You can also eliminate some answers using the rules.

B is wrong because rule four says that petrels are lectured on in Gladwyn Hall.

D is wrong because rule four says that sandpipers go before oystercatchers. So sandpipers can't go fifth.

E is wrong because rule five says that terns are before petrels. So terns can't go fifth.

C is slightly trickier to eliminate. If rails are fifth and in Howard Auditorium, then we know the placement of both Hs:

$$\frac{}{G} \quad \frac{}{G} \quad \frac{}{G} \quad \frac{}{H} \quad \frac{R}{H}$$

Rule four says that sandpipers have to be in Howard Auditorium. But rule four *also* says that sandpipers must be before oystercatchers.

That's not possible on this diagram. The only H where we can put sandpipers is in slot 4, and that leave no room to place sandpipers ahead of oystercatchers.

Question 23

This question places sandpipers third. Let's do that and see what happens. Remember, rule 4 says that sandpipers are in Howard Auditorium:

$$\frac{}{G} \quad \frac{}{} \quad \frac{S}{H} \quad \frac{}{} \quad \frac{O}{}$$

I also placed O to the right of S, as a reminder that rule 4 says that O comes after S.

So far, there are two Hs and one G on the diagram. Rule 3 says that there are three Gs, so we have to make the other two slots G:

$$\frac{}{G} \quad \frac{}{G} \quad \frac{S}{H} \quad \frac{}{H} \quad \frac{O}{G}$$

This diagram easily eliminates **A-C.**

A is wrong because O has to be after S. So O can't go second.

B and **C** are wrong because in this diagram the Hs are third and fourth, not second or fifth.

This diagram proves that **D** is possible:

$$\frac{R}{G} \quad \frac{T}{G} \quad \frac{S}{H} \quad \frac{O}{H} \quad \frac{P}{G}$$

D is **CORRECT.**

That diagram should also make clear why **E** is wrong. Rule five says that P is after T. So if T is fourth, then P has to go fifth.

But we also know that O has to go fourth or fifth, because rule four says that O is after S. So If we placed T fourth, then T, P and O would have to go in fourth and fifth. There's no space for that.

Section IV - Logical Reasoning

Question 1

QUESTION TYPE: Strengthen

CONCLUSION: We can't be certain enough to justify punishing the auto repair shop.

REASONING: There is some evidence that the auto shop is responsible for the pollution. But the penalty is very severe.

ANALYSIS: We're trying to judge whether the auto shop is responsible: should we convict them, or not? The argument says that stronger evidence is needed, because the penalty is harsh.

We need a principle that says this is correct. So the right answer will say that we *should* require strong evidence in order to impose harsh punishments. Principle questions are about what 'should' happen.

Answers B, C and E are about how to set a penalty for a crime. That's irrelevant. The penalty for this crime is already set.

A note on logical errors: did you *feel* that the auto shop was at fault? There's very little proof. 'Some' evidence 'suggests' the auto body shop is guilty. If you instantly decided the auto body shop was guilty, then that's a mental error you need to eliminate.

A. **CORRECT.** This matches what the stimulus said. The penalty is severe, so this answer tells us that we *should* wait for stronger evidence.
B. This tells us how severely you ought to punish crimes. But the stimulus was about whether we could conclude that the auto shop was guilty.
C. Same as B. This is about how to *set* the penalty for a crime. But we are trying to decide whether the auto shop is guilty. The penalty is already set.
D. No one has confessed. This is irrelevant. Admission of guilt is just a factor that *might* let us avoiding debating whether we have enough evidence to convict the auto body shop.
E. This tells you how to set a penalty. It doesn't tell you how to know whether someone is guilty.

Question 2

QUESTION TYPE: Most Strongly Supported

FACTS: Lots of nursing home residents suffer from depression. A study found that those who bond with pets are less likely to have depression.

ANALYSIS: We know *one* thing. Pets helped reduce depression.

That doesn't mean pets are the best method. Nor does it mean that pets will completely solve the problem. Likewise, we can't conclude that pets are essential to solving the problem.

We just know that pets help. They're solving a problem. Presumably, the people in nursing homes lack personal bonds, and pets help make up for that.

A. Careful. Maybe depression is a serious problem for everyone, not just nursing home residents. The question didn't compare nursing home residents to any other groups.
B. This goes too far. The question only told us that pets *help*. The question didn't compare pets to any other methods: maybe human companionship is even more effective.
C. **CORRECT.** This is fairly well supported. If you form a personal bond with a pet, then you have a new companion. The fact that pets reduce depression show that nursing home residents may be lacking companionship.
D. This goes too far. There might be people who are happy without animal companions. For instance, maybe people with many human companions don't need pets in order to be happy.
E. This goes too far. We know that pets *helped*. That doesn't mean they can eliminate the problem entirely.

Question 3

QUESTION TYPE: Flawed Reasoning

CONCLUSION: Only funny ads work well.

REASONING: Funny ads hold people's attention. Ads only work if they hold your attention.

ANALYSIS: Funny ads are *sufficient* to hold your attention. But other ads could also hold your attention – the stimulus didn't show that funniness is *necessary*.

You can diagram this if you'd like. There are two conditional statements that don't link up:

Funny → holds attention
Effective → holds attention

A. **CORRECT.** Maybe emotional ads can also hold people's attention. Then funny ads wouldn't be the only kind that could be effective.
B. The argument doesn't do this. The second sentence says that funny ads attract *and* hold your attention.
C. I found this very tempting. The argument implies that funny ads are effective, when all we know is that funny ads meet a *necessary* condition for effectiveness.

   So why isn't this right? It's because the main point of the conclusion is that funny ads are the *only* effective ads i.e. that no other ads can be effective. So A is the best answer. Though there is a case to be made that this answer is also right and that the question is flawed.
D. The stimulus uses "effective" the same way each time. To pick this type of answer, you have to say what the two different definitions of effective are.
E. The stimulus didn't even talk about the purpose of an advertisement. An answer can't be the flaw if it didn't happen.

Question 4

QUESTION TYPE: Strengthen

CONCLUSION: We shouldn't be concerned by stories about people getting sick after vaccination.

REASONING: Millions of people get vaccinated every year. We can expect that some will get sick afterwards by coincidence.

ANALYSIS: The doctor has shown that the illnesses *could* be caused by coincidence. To strengthen his argument, we should show evidence that helps prove that the illnesses *are* due only to coincidence.

The right answer does this by showing that there is no increased risk of illness following vaccination. That's pretty convincing.

A. This may weaken the argument. If illness only follows new vaccines, then maybe the vaccines weren't properly tested and they *do* cause illness.
B. This tells us whether or not to vaccinate people. It doesn't show whether vaccines are safe.
C. **CORRECT.** Suppose this wasn't true. Imagine 50 people a day get sick on average, but 600 people get sick the day after being vaccinated. That would imply that vaccines do increase risk. This answer eliminates that scenario – 50 people a day get sick the day before vaccinations, and 50 the day after. There's no obvious increased risk.
D. This doesn't tell us whether or not the vaccines *caused* the health problems.
E. If anything, this answer shows that vaccines can be dangerous. They make at least a few people sick. We're trying to prove that vaccines *don't* make people sick!

Question 5

QUESTION TYPE: Agreement

ARGUMENTS: Sharita says that there are a lot of stray cats, because people don't neuter their cats. She thinks that people *should* neuter their cats.

Chad says that stray cats cause disease, and that people shouldn't feed them.

ANALYSIS: Both Sharita and Chad agree that stray cats are a problem. Both of them would like fewer stray cats. Sharita would achieve this goal by having people neuter their pets. Chad would reduce the number of stray cats by having people not feed them.

All four wrong answers mentions thing that Sharita doesn't talk about. So we can't know whether Sharita would agree.

Notice that this is an *agreement* question. On past LSATs, most questions with two speakers were *disagreement* questions. Now the LSAC is including both agreement questions and disagreement questions fairly regularly – make sure to read the question stems carefully. I got a question wrong once because I chose a "disagree" answer on an agreement question.

A. Sharita doesn't mention feeding stray cats.
B. **CORRECT.** Sharita strongly implies this – otherwise why would she recommend neutering? Neutering reduces the number of cats.

Chad lists the ways that stray cats cause problems, and he recommends not feeding them. So presumably he agrees that there are too many.

There is some small amount of doubt whether they agree – Sharita isn't explicit in saying that there ought to be fewer strays. But this is just a 'most supports' question, so doubt is allowed.
C. Sharita doesn't mention whether stray cats pose a risk to anyone.
D. Sharita doesn't mention disease.
E. Sharita doesn't mention feeding stray cats.

Question 6

QUESTION TYPE: Necessary Assumption

CONCLUSION: Most people that embezzle or commit bribery will be caught.

REASONING: The more times you commit a crime, the more likely you are to be caught.

ANALYSIS: The first two sentences are just filler. The key here is that the more times you embezzle, the more likely you are to be caught.

There's a problem though. The argument doesn't say whether embezzlers will continue embezzling. Just because someone is confident doesn't mean that they will keep committing crimes. The conclusion is that most embezzlers will be caught, but maybe most people embezzle once and then drop it.

Note: this is a rare case where a "most" answer is correct on a necessary assumption question. Negating "most" moves from 51% to 50%, which isn't normally logically significant. But the conclusion of this argument was about "most" embezzlers.

A. **CORRECT.** If most people don't embezzle repeatedly, then the detective's evidence doesn't support his argument. It's still possible that most embezzlers would be caught (say, on the first try). But they would not be caught because of the reasoning in the detective's argument. That's why this is necessary to the argument.
Negation: Half or less of those who embezzle do so repeatedly.
B. Confidence was just a sideshow to the argument. The main point is that the odds of being caught go up as the criminal commits more crimes.
C. The conclusion is simply that most embezzlers will be caught. Other crimes don't matter – who care if it's even easier to catch car thieves?
D. This doesn't *have* to be true. Maybe even careful repeat offenders have patterns that make it easy to catch them if they embezzle often enough.
E. The conclusion is that most embezzlers would be caught. So the argument would be *stronger* if some embezzlers were caught the first time!

Question 7

QUESTION TYPE: Paradox

PARADOX: When grain prices rise, grain fed beef gets expensive much faster than bread does.

ANALYSIS: The first step on paradox questions is to figure out why the situation is confusing. It's odd that beef gets expensive so much *faster* than bread does. Bread is mostly made of grain, so we would expect it to get expensive faster.

Note that this question shows how you're allowed to use outside knowledge to make warranted assumptions. Everyone knows that bread is made from grains – the question doesn't need to say this explicitly.

So in fact you *must* use outside knowledge to answer this question. It's a warranted assumption to say that bread is made from grains. What you're *not* allowed to do with outside knowledge is use it to contradict the argument, or add a fact that many people would disagree with.

A. Duh. Every employer tries to reduce labor costs. Unlike the correct answer, this answer doesn't say whether labor costs are *actually* low. Employers could fail to reduce costs, despite their best efforts.
B. Everyone knows that beef is expensive and bread is cheap. The point of the stimulus was that the *change* in the price of meat was very large compared to the change in the price of bread.
C. **CORRECT.** This shows that grain prices have only a small impact on bread prices, whereas grain prices greatly affect the price of cattle feed and hence the price of cattle.
D. This explains why beef got more expensive. It doesn't explain why beef got expensive so much faster than bread.
E. So what? This just tells us a couple of interesting facts about bread and meat purchasing. We have no idea how these facts influence *prices*.

Question 8

QUESTION TYPE: Method of Reasoning

CONCLUSION: Kathy says that the two drugs probably have different side effects.

REASONING: Kathy says that the two drugs are chemically different, even though the drugs achieve their effects through the same physiological mechanisms.

ANALYSIS: Kathy doesn't disagree with Mark's facts. Instead, she points out a relevant fact that Mark ignored, and uses this to disagree with Mark's conclusion.

A. Kathy didn't mention any drug's safety record. This answer simply didn't happen.
B. This answer describes an argument by analogy, where you talk about *something else* in order to prove a point. But Kathy made no analogy – she just talked about the drugs themselves.
C. Kathy didn't mention any studies. How could this possibly be the right answer?
D. *Which* fundamental principles of medicine? Kathy didn't mention any.
E. **CORRECT.** Here we go. Mark made an analogy between Zokaz and Qualzan in order to prove that Qualzan is risky. Kathy points out that Zokaz and Qualzan are chemically different. This breaks the analogy.

Question 9

QUESTION TYPE: Flawed Reasoning

CONCLUSION: We are an environmentally responsible company.

REASONING: We pollute less than we used to, and there are no methods we could use that produce zero pollution. Environmentally responsible organizations pollute the least they can.

ANALYSIS: I'll illustrate this with numbers. Suppose 100 is the most pollution you can produce, and 0 is the least. I'll make an example that fits the CEO's facts, yet shows that his company is a horrible polluter.

The CEO says that he pollutes less than he used to, and there are no methods that let him pollute at zero. So maybe the CEO's company used to pollute at 95, and now they pollute at 93. Whoop-de-do.

An environmentally responsible organization will pollute the least that it can. If there is a method that would let the CEO's company pollute at 20, then they're not being responsible, even though they're better than they used to be.

A. The CEO didn't say this. He said that *currently* there are no zero pollution methods. So maybe the company is doing all that it can at present, even if better methods will be available later.
B. Huh? This is a completely different error. It's like saying "ice cream makes you fat, so donuts don't". The CEO didn't make this error.
C. This is a different error. It's like saying "No, I wasn't rude in the restaurant. Therefore, I am never rude". The CEO is only talking about a specific criticism: whether or not the company is environmentally responsible.
D. The final sentence didn't say that the company *attempted* to reduce pollution. The CEO says that the company *did* reduce pollution.
E. **CORRECT.** See my analysis above. It's true that the company can't produce zero pollution, but maybe they can still try harder to produce *less* pollution than they currently do. If so, they're not being responsible.

Question 10

QUESTION TYPE: Necessary Assumption

CONCLUSION: Suppression of the immune system can cause or worsen gum disease.

REASONING: You're more likely to have gum disease if you refuse to think about problems. Stress affects the immune system.

ANALYSIS: This question makes several big leaps. First of all, the first sentence doesn't talk about stress. So it's not clear that solving problems directly will reduce stress.

Secondly, the argument has, at best, established a correlation between stress/immune suppression and gum disease. It's possible that there's some other reason that those who solve problems quickly get less gum disease.

A. This is totally off base. The argument didn't even mention whether gum disease is painful.
B. **CORRECT.** If refusing to think about problems *doesn't* cause stress, then there's no link between stress and gum disease.
   Negation: Refusing to think about problems doesn't cause stress.
C. Actually, the argument implied that people who address problems quickly and directly *don't* feel stress.
   If you want to get technical, I suppose you can have a stressful life without succumbing to stress, but that's irrelevant. The argument was talking about the stress that people feel.
D. This shows an alternate reason that people who address problems get less gum disease. This *weakens* the argument if it's true.
E. It doesn't matter *why* people avoid addressing problems. It only matters that they suffer stress because they avoid problems.

LSAT 70 - SECTION IV, LR

Question 11

QUESTION TYPE: Flawed Reasoning

CONCLUSION: The fruits tested stay fresh better in cooler temperatures.

REASONING: The class tested three temperatures. The coolest temperature worked best.

ANALYSIS: The class tested a very limited range of temperatures. They forget that temperatures can be *much* colder than 10 degrees.

Their conclusion is that colder is always better. That's absurd – it would mean that fruits stay fresh the longest at absolute zero.

Maybe 10 degrees is the *ideal* temperature. Warmer is worse, but so is colder.

A. The conclusion was only about the fruits tested, not all fruit. If you chose this, you need to be more precise about what conclusions say.
B. The argument didn't say that coolness is the only factor that mattered. The conclusion said that cooler temperature leads to longer-lasting freshness. That kind of language *doesn't* mean that all other factors are irrelevant.
   If I say "The more you study, the higher you'll score on the LSAT", it's implied that I mean "....other things equal". Obviously you'll perform worse if you don't sleep the night before the test in order to study eight extra hours.
C. **CORRECT.** The class only proved that, of the three temperatures, colder was better. But it's possible that very cold temperatures would be worse. The class didn't test -50 degrees.
D. The stimulus didn't mention a thermometer. And we know from outside experience that thermometers are generally reliable enough to indicate that 10 degrees is cooler than 20 degrees. We can assume that *if* the class used a thermometer, then the thermometer fine, unless we're given evidence to the contrary.
E. If I say "coolness helps preserve fruit" then that fact is my conclusion. I don't need to explain it. An explanation of why it's true could require 500 pages of plant biology.

Question 12

QUESTION TYPE: Weaken

CONCLUSION: We won't face a plague of water shortages in the near future.

REASONING: We only use a small portion of our fresh water.

ANALYSIS: If you live in a desert area, you might see the flaw. Water isn't distributed evenly.

I live in Canada. We've got tons of water. More than we know what to do with. Other countries aren't so lucky, and they're short on water already. With more population growth, they'll face more shortages. It's not that easy to share water. You can export it in bulk, but you can't make it rain in other countries.

A. The conclusion says that we'll have shortages "*unless* population growth trends change". So this possibility of error is already accounted for.
B. **CORRECT.** This points out the possibility that we could have water shortages in some regions even if most regions have more than enough water. And this is a real problem – many arid regions face water shortages even at current population levels.
C. So what? Apparently we're only using a small portion of our water, so water conservation doesn't seem like it needs to be a priority. If you thought "some regions don't have water and thus need to conserve"....well, answer B is the answer that address that concern. Answer C doesn't address differences between regions.
D. The key word in this answer is *eventually*. The argument only disagrees with the prediction that we'll face shortages in the *near future*.
E. So? I see no reason to expect that water usage rates in different industries will increase at the same speed. And the key fact in the stimulus is that we're using only a small portion of our water. This answer doesn't tell us that we'll run out of water even with massively increased agricultural usage.

71

Question 13

QUESTION TYPE: Paradox

PARADOX: The industrial revolution increased productivity by centralizing decision making. But recently, a bunch of already productive companies have increased their productivity by decreasing centralization.

ANALYSIS: The paradox is that centralization seems to both help and hurt productivity. We need to explain why certain companies improved productivity by decentralizing.

The industrial revolution was 200 years ago. It's possible that we've begun to reach the limits of centralization.

A. This is just a fact about most companies. This doesn't explain how some other companies managed to improve their productivity through decentralization.
B. Great – those employees must be happy! But this doesn't *explain* why decentralization worked.
C. Robots don't explain decentralization. Maybe robots require central control.
D. The stimulus was very specific. It talked about already productive companies i.e. those that *had* already learned the lessons of the industrial revolution and centralized. We need to explain why some of *those* companies improved productivity by decentralizing.
In other words, who cares about the companies mentioned in this answer choice? They're not the companies that we're talking about.
E. **CORRECT.** This explains it. The companies in question are already productive. This answer says that those productive companies can *only* become even more productive if they decentralize a bit and give employees influence.

Question 14

QUESTION TYPE: Must Be True

FACTS:

1. Epic poetry's main function is to transmit values.
2. Epic poems do this by presenting heroes as role models.
3. People get meaning in their lives from imitating these role models.

ANALYSIS: The most important thing on must be true questions is to have a clear idea of the facts. Usually the right answer will combine two or more of them.

A. The stimulus was about *epic* poetry. This answer is about all poetry. Maybe epic poetry is an unimportant part of poetry in general.
B. **CORRECT.** This combines facts 1 and 2.
C. Careful. The *transmission* of values is not done by explicit discussion, but that doesn't mean values aren't set forth explicitly. e.g. "The hero was brave, strong and noble". In my example, I didn't discuss the hero's values, but they are set forth explicitly, for you to mimic. Be brave.
D. This sounds good, but the problem is "many groups of people". The stimulus doesn't say whether many groups of people are exposed to epic poetry any more.
E. This confuses sufficient for necessary. Yes, all epic poetry presents heroes as role models. But plenty of other things present heroes as role models too....Disney movies for instance.

Question 15

QUESTION TYPE: Principle – Strengthen

CONCLUSION: The proposal is morally right.

REASONING: There's a proposal to confiscate burglars' wages. The money would go to a fund for burglary victims.

ANALYSIS: Principle – Strengthen questions are similar to sufficient assumption questions. The reasoning will be a bunch of facts about an idea. The conclusion will be that the idea is morally good.

Just look for an answer that says that one or more of the facts from the reasoning helps prove that something is morally good.

A. This tells you what to do *if* you steal money from a burglar or receive money stolen from a burglar. This answer doesn't tell you *whether* you should steal from a burglar.
   Also, the money in the argument will go to a general fund for victims of burglary. So money taken from a burglar won't necessarily go to his specific victims.

B. This answer only places an obligation on burglars. That doesn't mean the Government has the right to force burglars to meet their obligations.

C. **CORRECT.** The government program has a good motive. This answer shows that the motive is relevant.
   To be clear, this isn't a sufficient assumption, it just strengthens the argument.

D. This sounds good, but it just gives us a *necessary* condition for justifying stealing. Necessary conditions *never* help prove a point.
   Suppose you're wondering if you can drive from NYC to LA, and you've got a map. If I say "you'll *only* get there if you have a map", have I helped you arrive? No! In fact, I've restricted you. Now, if you lose your map, you're lost. Before I added the condition, the map was just a nice bonus.

E. This contradicts the argument. We're trying to say that stealing from burglars *is* justified.

Question 16

QUESTION TYPE: Identify The Conclusion

CONCLUSION: It's false to think that unrelieved heartburn will probably cause esophageal cancer.

REASONING: Only those with Barrett's esophagus have a higher risk of cancer due to heartburn. Only 5% of those who get heartburn have Barrett's esophagus.

ANALYSIS: Any time an author gives their opinion about the truth, it's almost certainly the conclusion.

So when the author says "this is simply false" it means that their conclusion is that they disagree with the first sentence.

This is a good argument, by the way. You might have thought that the author admitted that heartburn can cause cancer. The author *did* admit this. But their conclusion is that heartburn isn't *likely* to cause cancer. "Likely" means "51% of the time or more" – it's a synonym for most. So 5% of the time isn't enough to make cancer risk "likely".

A. This is evidence that supports the conclusion that cancer risk isn't likely.

B. This is evidence that supports the idea that those with Barrett's esophagus *do* have an increased risk of cancer.

C. **CORRECT.** The first sentence made the claim that heartburn is likely to cause cancer. The second sentence shows that the author disagrees. When the author presents a claim and disagrees with it, that will be their conclusion.

D. This is just a fact that allows the author to make his argument. If advertisements weren't making this claim, the author would have nothing to talk about. But the conclusion is that the author *disagrees* with these commercials.

E. This isn't even true, necessarily. It's possible that TV advertisements are so targeted that the ads are mostly seen by those with Barrett's esophagus. So the ads would be relevant to the viewers. This targeting would be possible with ads on Hulu for example – your web browser knows a *lot* about you.

Question 17

QUESTION TYPE: Parallel Reasoning

CONCLUSION: At least some halogen lamps are well crafted.

REASONING: Anything on display at Furniture Labyrinth is well crafted. Some halogen lamps are on display at Furniture labyrinth.

- Labyrinth display → Well Crafted
- Labyrinth display SOME halogen lamps

ANALYSIS: This is a good argument. It gives one conditional statement, and then a "some" statement which connects with the sufficient condition of the conditional.

Anytime a "some" statement connects with a sufficient condition, you can make a new some statement. Here's an example:

Cat → Tail
Cat SOME Brown
Conclusion: Brown SOME Tail (i.e. some brown things have tails)

A. This answer has a *chance* of storms. In the stimulus we *knew* that lamps were displayed.
B. **CORRECT.** This is a good argument. It matches the structure of the stimulus exactly.

    Written by Melissa → Disturbing
    Written by Melissa SOME sonnets
    Conclusion: Sonnets SOME Disturbing.
C. This is a bad argument. Gianna *can* get her car worked on, but that doesn't mean that she *will*. Also, car shops are *capable* of good work, but that doesn't mean Gianna will inevitably receive good work.
D. Maybe the lakes teem with healthy *trout,* but all the minnows are unhealthy. To be correct, this answer would have had to say that *all* fish in the nearby lakes are healthy.
E. This is a good argument, but it doesn't match the structure. The stimulus concluded that at least *some* lamps were well crafted. This answer concludes that *all* the cornmeal is healthful.

Question 18

QUESTION TYPE: Most Strongly Supported

FACTS:

1. Managers usually don't benefit from flexibility.
2. This might be because most managers already have flexibility.
3. Normal workers benefit from flexibility. They are happier and more productive.
4. The benefits diminish over time, and it's possible to make schedules too flexible.

ANALYSIS: It's hard to prephrase "most strongly supported" questions. The best approach is to get a clear idea of the facts, then look at each answer quickly in order to eliminate a few.

When you're down to 1-2 answers, check them against the stimulus to be sure they're supported by a combination of facts.

A. This is very tempting. Regular workers benefit, so shouldn't we expect managers to benefit from flexible schedules, if they didn't already have them? Maybe. But managers are different from workers. Maybe there's a *reason* these managers don't have flexible schedules – their jobs might require them to be at work during certain hours.

    So we can't be sure that managers without flexibility would benefit the same way that regular workers do. E is a better answer.
B. This *contradicts* the argument. It's a warranted assumption that most workers are not managers, so we *can* expect flexibility to improve the overall morale of the workforce.
C. Hard to say. Fact 3 doesn't say how much productivity improves. And fact 4 says that the improvement is worse over the long run.
D. If you picked this, you probably misread fact 2. Managers already have flexibility. *That's* why further flexibility doesn't help them. But managers may benefit from the flexibility they already have.
E. **CORRECT.** If we assume that the typical worker is not a manager (a reasonable assumption), then managers are not a good indicator of how the typical worker will benefit from flexibility.

Question 19

QUESTION TYPE: Weaken

CONCLUSION: The respondents may have been biased in favor of Lopez.

REASONING: Most people who watched the debate said that Lopez argued better. Lopez eventually won.

ANALYSIS: First, you must understand what the argument is saying. Suppose that Lopez won the election with 60% of the votes.

In that case, it's likely that most debate viewers already liked Lopez. If 60% of people watching the debate liked Lopez, then it's hardly surprising if most people said that he won.

And that's the basis of the right answer. If we know instead that most of the audience did *not* support Lopez, then that means he must have convinced some people during the debate.

A. The question is talking about those who *did* watch the debate. We need to know how many of them supported Lopez. It's possible very few people watched the debate, maybe only 20%. That would mean that most supported of both candidates didn't watch. This answer tells us nothing.

B. This just adds confusion. If most members of the live audience liked Tanner, why did Lopez do better on television? This has no clear impact on the argument.

C. This is very, very tempting. But let's play with the numbers. Let's say only 15% of people voted for Tanner, and 20% of those watching the debate voted for Tanner. That means that those who watched the debate were more likely than the general public to vote for Tanner. Yet most of the audience would vote for Lopez.

D. **CORRECT.** This shows that a majority of the audience was against Lopez, pre-debate. But after the debate, most said that Lopez won. That's evidence that Lopez was a good debater.

E. So what? Suppose Lopez won with 51% of votes, and 51% of those who saw the debate supported Lopez. That's still a bias in favor of Lopez.

Question 20

QUESTION TYPE: Necessary Assumption

CONCLUSION: The data can't explain the origin of the prohibitions.

REASONING: Data show that certain food prohibitions were useful. But ancient peoples who made the prohibitions didn't have access to that data.

ANALYSIS: This is a tricky flaw. I'll illustrate with an example. Let's say you're with a group of people, and you come across two doors, A and B.

Some people from your group go through each door, and return. They can't remember what happened. But the people who went through door A came back with good food, fine clothing and bountiful treasure. The people who went through door B came back moaning in pain, and died shortly thereafter.

You don't know what happened beyond the doors, but wouldn't you choose to go through door A instead of door B?

Now suppose that scientists later studied the doors. They found that through door A there was a generous wizard, and that through door B there was an evil sorcerer. Obviously, the group's decision to go through door A *can* be explained in terms of this data, even though at the time the group only had access to the effects of the wizards, and not the full data.

In other words, you can repeat a good decision without knowing why it works. The original peoples might have seen that a food was causing harm. They wouldn't know why – only future data could explain the harm. But the people nonetheless banned the harmful food, and thus the later data can explain the decision.

I've made this explanation longer because I wanted to give you a full explanation of the situation. It's one of the most subtle that I've seen.

(Answers on next page)

A. CORRECT. The negation of this answer says that we don't need to worry about what the people originally knew. It completely wrecks the argument – maybe we *can* explain the prohibitions in terms of our data, even if the original people didn't have access to the data.

Negation: The origins of a food prohibition don't need to be explained with reference to the understanding that the people who adopted the prohibition had.

B. The stimulus didn't say whether any of the food prohibitions were contradictory. This is totally irrelevant.

C. Negate this and you get: there's a correlation between the social usefulness of a food prohibition and the nutritional value of that food.

That has no impact on the argument. The argument didn't talk about how nutritional food was.

D. "Often" is a synonym for most. So the negation of this answer is "half or less of the time, the origins of a food prohibition are forgotten within a few generations". The change from "most" to "half" has no effect on the argument. "Most" statements tend to be useless for necessary assumption questions.

This isn't relevant in any case. The argument is about *what* the original reasons were, not *how long* they were remembered.

E. The negation is "the originators of the prohibitions generally *didn't* have a non-technical understanding of the medical impacts of the prohibitions ".

This negated version *helps* the argument, by showing that the medical function can't help explain the origins.

Question 21

QUESTION TYPE: Must Be True

FACTS:

1. Published book → literary agent submission OR manuscript request
2. Serious attention → Renowned figure OR Requested manuscript after review of proposal

Note: The first sentence has a most statement. I didn't draw it, because it doesn't link up with anything. Meanwhile, I combined the two facts in the first sentence into fact 1 above.

ANALYSIS: Imagine this as a real world situation. How does a book get published? The publisher gets interested somehow and gets a manuscript. If they like it, they publish it. So, the first step is the manuscript. The second step is publication:

1. Manuscript: Renowned, or requested
2. Published: Literary agent, or requested

So requests are an important part of the system. You can only sidestep a request by being renowned, and then by having your literary agent submit.

A. Hard to say. Maybe most unrequested manuscripts come from renowned figures.

B. The first sentence talks about publishing. We're not told if most books are fiction. The renowned author reference is just there to confuse you: renowned authors were mentioned in the *second* sentence, and not in reference to publishing.

C. The second sentence describes when a book will get careful attention. That sentence never mentions whether fiction is an important factor.

D. Literary agents are only mentioned in the *first* sentence, in reference to publishing. The stimulus doesn't say whether literary agents are a major factor in attracting careful attention. If the publishing house requested a manuscript from a writer then the publishing house might give it very serious attention even without an agent.

E. CORRECT. A manuscript needs serious consideration to be published. If the manuscript was unrequested, the the author needs renown to get attention.

Question 22

QUESTION TYPE: Sufficient Assumption

CONCLUSION: Most of the drinking water will become polluted.

REASONING:
1. No budget for inspectors → Federal standards not met in most dairies
2. We don't have a budget for inspectors

ANALYSIS: The evidence lets us prove that most large dairies won't meet federal standards. But that doesn't prove that water will become polluted. We need to connect the evidence to the conclusion.

As with all sufficient assumption questions, just look at what you already know, and look where you want to go. Then add a new statement that connects what you know to where you need to go:

No budget → standards not met → water polluted

A. We're trying to conclude that the water *will* become polluted. This answer shows us a way that water *won't* become polluted.
Note that this statement can't tell us what would happen if dairies *don't* meet standards: negating the sufficient never tells you anything.
B. This is very tempting. But this answer only says that without inspectors we can't keep *all* drinking water clean. Maybe we can still keep 99.9% of it clean without more inspectors. The conclusion was that *most* water would be polluted.
C. This is close, but it gives us a *necessary* condition for water becoming polluted. Necessary conditions never prove that something will happen. We need a *sufficient* condition for water becoming polluted.
D. **CORRECT.** We already know that most large dairies won't meet federal standards, because we don't have the budget for new inspectors. This answer uses that information to let us prove that therefore most water will be polluted.
E. Close, but not quite. We know that inspectors won't be hired, and therefore *most* large dairies won't meet federal standards. But we don't know if *all* large dairies will fail to meet standards.

Question 23

QUESTION TYPE: Flawed Parallel Reasoning

CONCLUSION: The Vegetaste Burger will probably be very successful.

REASONING:
1. Successful product → Massive ad campaign
2. Vegetaste will have a massive ad campaign

ANALYSIS: The president gives us a single conditional statement, then tells us that Vegetaste meets the *necessary* condition of that statement.

A necessary condition never proves anything. It's as if I said that because something has a tail, it's a cat.

So we need another argument with one conditional statement and the necessary condition as evidence. Then the argument should incorrectly conclude the sufficient condition.

A. This is a silly argument. It's like saying "Barack Obama must be the president of some other country, because most people in America are not president". But this is a flaw of numbers, not the flaw made in the stimulus.
B. We can say that if you work at Coderight, you *probably* have ten years experience. Donna will probably meet this sufficient condition, but the argument concludes that she will *certainly* have the experience. So this is a bad argument. But it doesn't reverse sufficient and necessary.
C. This is actually a pretty good argument. If 95% of Acme's workers are factory workers, and 95% of them oppose the merger, then at least 90.25% of Acme's workers oppose the merger.
D. **CORRECT.** This mirrors the structure:
President → Ph.D
Robert has a Ph.D

We can't expect Robert to become president just because he meets the necessary condition. Maybe Robert is a down-on-his-luck hobo with a Ph.D
E. This is a pretty good argument. Evidence from the past can let us make probabilistic predictions about the future.

77

Question 24

QUESTION TYPE: Role in Argument

CONCLUSION: Life may be able to begin under lots of difficult conditions.

REASONING: Earth is 4.6 billion years old. We found bacteria 3.5 billion years old. These bacteria had a long evolutionary history, indicating that they must have appeared during the harsh conditions following the Earth's formation.

ANALYSIS: The bacteria are 3.5 billion years old. But they had a long evolutionary history.

The question asks: why does the argument mention this fact? Well, it proves that the ancestors of the bacteria were very, very old. So old that they must have been around in the early day of Earth's history, when conditions were rough.

This lends support to the conclusion that life can arise under difficult conditions.

———————

A. There *is* support for the claim that the bacteria had a long evolutionary history: they were complex. And this fact doesn't *illustrate* the conclusion (i.e. show an example of). Instead, this fact *supports* the conclusion.
B. There *is* support for the claim that the bacteria have a long history: they are complex.
C. **CORRECT.** The support for the claim is that the bacteria were complex. This is why we think they had a long evolutionary history. And this fact about history supports the claim that the bacteria evolved under difficult conditions. That in turn supports the conclusion that life all around the universe could evolve in difficult conditions.
D. Nope. There is some support provided to this claim. But the claim about evolution also supports another claim: life evolved under difficult conditions.
E. It's true that the claim about the bacteria's history supports a conclusion: the bacteria must have evolved during a difficult period. But this conclusion *does* support the main conclusion. The final sentence says "this suggests", referring to the previous sentence.

Question 25

QUESTION TYPE: Necessary Assumption

CONCLUSION: Astronomers thought that the stars were within a few million miles of the Earth.

REASONING: The astronomers thought that the stars moved around the Earth. If the stars were very far away, they would have to move very fast.

ANALYSIS: The flaw is *not* thinking that the stars revolve around the Earth. That's just context to set up the situation. You can reason correctly from false hypotheticals, i.e. "*If* unicorns exist, then....".

The conclusion is the second sentence ("They concluded"). The astronomers think the stars can't be far away, otherwise stars would move very fast. So what....why is it a problem for stars to move fast? The astronomers only *implied* that great speeds were a problem. If an argument implies something but doesn't state it, then that is an *assumption*.

You can use some outside knowledge on this question. Stars appear in the same position each night. Everyone agrees on this – it's why sailors could navigate by the stars. It's why astronomers thought stars would have to travel fast each night.

———————

A. The astronomers were assuming that the stars *do* revolve around the Earth. This talks about what happens if they *don't*. It's as though you're planning for how to take the LSAT, and I make an argument about what happens if you *weren't* required to take the LSAT. Irrelevant.
B. Why would it matter if one star moved 0.00001 mph faster than another star?
C. If you negate this, you get "Earth remains motionless while the stars revolve around it". That doesn't contradict the astronomers.
D. **CORRECT.** The astronomers' *only* reason for saying the stars couldn't be far away was that the stars would move quickly if they were far away. **Negation:** Stars move at very great speeds.
E. If you negate this, you get "stars more than a million miles away could *not* reappear in the same position". This strengthens the argument: the stars have to be even closer. The astronomers were predicting a maximum, not a minimum.

Question 26

QUESTION TYPE: Method of Reasoning

CONCLUSION: People appreciate paintings for more than being exact replicas of scenes.

REASONING: If people only cared about replicating scenes, then photography would have completely eliminated paintings.

ANALYSIS: The first few lines are just context. I've summarized the reasoning above.

This is a good argument. We all know that a camera can replicate a scene more accurately and more quickly than a painter can.

Yet people still paint, and people still enjoy new paintings. So there must be some other things that people like about paintings.

A couple of the answers mention that the argument is a defense of people's taste. It isn't. The argument may perhaps defend abstract impressionism, but the argument isn't defending the fact that people like more than realism in paintings. That's just a fact that the argument wants to prove.

A. The stimulus doesn't mention "what most people appreciate". This couldn't possibly be the right answer. Also, the conclusion is not about an abstract principle. The conclusion is about what people appreciate in paintings.

B. What aesthetic principle? The stimulus doesn't mention any. And the argument isn't *defending* people's tastes. It's merely describing them.

C. The stimulus is talking about the present, not about history. And it's not explaining the present. Instead, the stimulus makes a claim about what's true in the present.

D. **CORRECT.** The historical fact is that photography hasn't displaced painting. The claim is that people like paintings for more than their ability to reproduce scenes.

E. The argument doesn't say that people are *right* to like paintings for more than their realism. This argument is not a defense of people's tastes.

Appendix: LR Questions By Type

Strengthen

Section I, #3
Section I, #25
Section IV, #1
Section IV, #4

Weaken

Section I, #16
Section IV, #12
Section IV, #19

Sufficient Assumption

Section I, #1
Section I, #7
Section IV, #22

Parallel Reasoning

Section I, #19
Section IV, #17

Flawed Parallel Reasoning

Section I, #10
Section IV, #23

Necessary Assumption

Section I, #13
Section I, #21
Section IV, #6
Section IV, #10
Section IV, #20
Section IV, #25

Method of Reasoning

Section IV, #8
Section IV, #26

Must Be True

Section I, #8
Section I, #22
Section I, #24
Section IV, #14
Section IV, #21

Most Strongly Supported

Section IV, #2
Section IV, #18

Paradox

Section I, #5
Section I, #12
Section IV, #7
Section IV, #13

Principle

Section I, #6
Section I, #14
Section I, #23
Section IV, #15

Identify The Conclusion

Section I, #18
Section IV, #16

Agreement

Section IV, #5

Point At Issue

Section I, #4

Role in Argument

Section I, #17
Section IV, #24

Argument Evaluation

Section I, #11

Flawed Reasoning

Section I, #2
Section I, #9
Section I, #15
Section I, #20
Section IV, #3
Section IV, #9
Section IV, #11

Thank You

First of all, thank you for buying this book. Writing these explanations has been the most satisfying work I have ever done. I sincerely hope they have been helpful to you, and I wish you success on the LSAT and as a lawyer.

If you left an Amazon review, you get an extra special thank you! I truly appreciate it. You're helping others discover Hacking The LSAT.

Thanks also to Anu Panil, who drew the diagrams for the logic games. Anu, thank you for making sense of the scribbles and scans I sent you. You are surely ready to master logic games after all the work you did.

Thanks to Alison Rayner, who helped me with the layout and designed the cover. If this book looks nice, she deserves credit. Alison caught many mistakes I would never have found by myself (any that remain are my own, of course).

Thanks to Ludovic Glorieux, who put up with me constantly asking him if a design change looked good or bad.

Finally, thanks to my parents, who remained broadly supportive despite me being crazy enough to leave law school to teach the LSAT. I love you guys.

About The Author

Graeme Blake lives in Montreal Canada. He first took the LSAT in June 2007, and scored a 177. It was love at first site. He taught the LSAT for Testmasters for a couple of years before going to the University of Toronto for law school.

Upon discovering that law was not for him, Graeme began working as an independent LSAT tutor. He teaches LSAT courses in Montreal for Ivy Global and tutors students from all around the world using Skype.

He publishes a series of LSAT guides and explanations under the title Hacking The LSAT. Versions of these explanations can be found at LSAT Blog, Cambridge LSAT and Zen of 180, as well as amazon.com.

Graeme is also the moderator of www.reddit.com/r/LSAT, Reddit's LSAT forum. He worked for a time with 7Sage LSAT.

Graeme finds it unusual to write in the third person to describe himself, but he recognizes the importance of upholding publishing traditions. He wonders if many people read about the author pages.

You can find him at www.lsathacks.com and www.reddit.com/r/LSAT.

Graeme encourages you to get in touch by email, his address is graeme@lsathacks.com. Or you can call 514-612-1526. He's happy to hear feedback or give advice.

Further Reading

I hope you liked this book. If you did, I'd be very grateful if you took two minutes to review it on amazon. People judge a book by its reviews, and if you review this book you'll help other LSAT students discover it.

Ok, so you've written a review and want to know what to do next.

The most important LSAT books are the preptests themselves. Many students think they have to read every strategy guide under the sun, but you'll learn the most simply from doing real LSAT questions and analyzing your mistakes.

At the time of writing, there are 70 official LSATs. The most recent ones are best, but if you've got a while to study I recommend doing every test from 19 or from 29 onwards.

This series (Hacking The LSAT) is a bit different from other LSAT prep books. This book is not a strategy guide.

Instead, my goal is to let you do what my own students get to do when they take lessons with me: review their work with the help of an expert.

These explanations show you a better way to approach questions, and exactly why answers are right or wrong.

If you found this book useful, here's the list of other books in the series:

- Hacking The LSAT: Full Explanations For LSATs 29-38, Volume I
- Hacking The LSAT: Full Explanations For LSATs 29-38, Volume II
- LSAT 66 Explanations (Hacking The LSAT Series)
- LSAT 67 Explanations (Hacking The LSAT Series)
- LSAT 68 Explanations (Hacking The LSAT Series)
- LSAT 69 Explanations (Hacking The LSAT Series)

Keep an eye out, as I'll be steadily publishing explanations for earlier LSATs, starting with LSAT 65 and moving backwards.

If you *are* looking for strategy guides, try Manhattan LSAT or Powerscore. Unlike other companies, they use real LSAT questions in their books.

I've written a longer piece on LSAT books on Reddit. It includes links to the best LSAT books and preptests. If you're serious about the LSAT and want the best materials, I strongly recommend you read it:

http://redd.it/uf4uh

(this is a shortlink that takes you to the correct page)

Review This Book

I'm going to assume that you found this book useful, and therefore I'm not out of line in asking for a small favor.

Review this book on amazon.com (or wherever you bought it). In return, I'll gladly answer any questions you've got about the LSAT.

Writing a review takes less than a minute, and it makes a BIG difference in how amazon displays my books. If you like this book and leave a review, then more LSAT students will find out about this book series.

Like I said, I'd gladly answer questions for you if you leave a review. Just send me an email, graeme@lsathacks.com, and include a link to your review.

I'd truly appreciate it. Thanks.

7219157R00048

Made in the USA
San Bernardino, CA
26 December 2013